GET PAID
TO RACE

JESS SHANAHAN

GET PAID TO RACE

First Published in 2018 by Compass-Publishing
www.compass-publishing.com

Printed in the United Kingdom by CMP Group Ltd

A catalogue version of the book can be found at the British Library

Designed by The Book Refinery Ltd
www.thebookrefinery.com

Contents

A Note from the Author

For the most part, I will be referring to you as the person searching for sponsorship, and usually as a racing driver. However, the content in this book is relevant whether you race a car, motorcycle, powerboat or something else entirely. Even other athletes may find some useful content in this book.

This book is also relevant if you run a race team, are parent to a racing driver, manage a driver or run a race series.

So, while I'll often refer to racing drivers for ease and consistency, I'm thinking about you all.

Introduction

Your Racing Mentor

I hated sales. I had a crap advertising sales job at a popular automotive classified site that I really didn't care about. The people were great, but cold calling was stressful and I was absolutely terrible at it.

I barely made sales, but the ones I did make were with people willing to chat on the phone, hammering home the point that building a rapport was important. The problem was, no one had ever taught me how to build a rapport; I was awkward and shy with no real people skills. I was not (and am not!) a natural salesperson.

We had certain key performance indicators (KPIs) to hit in terms of calls made and sales landed; I coasted through but rarely hit targets. I was pretty sure sales wasn't for me and was relieved when I got made redundant.

From there, I went into PR and was working with clients who I loved and believed in. I soon realised that selling a story to a magazine or newspaper took similar sales skills, but I wasn't terrible at it. Because I was excited about the brands I worked with, it was so much easier to talk about them to the journalists

I was calling. Again, building a relationship and rapport with those journalists was important for getting the most coverage.

Then, I quit my job and decided to pursue a career in writing for other people. I never even thought of the daily hustle to find clients as sales, but it was. Again, because I cared and believed in my business, it was easy to sell it to people. That being said, as soon as I upped my sales game, I brought in more business and made more money.

In learning to network, sell myself and sell my business, I unlocked something within me that was confident and business-savvy. While the deeper sales process of questioning people, discovering their goals, selling the benefits, qualifying the buyer and asking closing questions was still a struggle, I was getting it.

When I moved into the exciting world of motorsport, I was tasked with getting sponsorship for a karter. How hard could it be, right? The first person I pitched to was a friend who owned a telecommunications business. He told me he'd sponsored karting before but hadn't really got anything back from it.

That made me think about the business benefits of sponsoring a racing driver. When I really thought about it, realistically, what was a business going to get from seeing its logo on a car?

From there, I changed my approach and worked with a few karters for whom I secured some small sponsorship deals, and we did good work for a few local businesses.

Since those early days of refining my sponsorship process, I've worked with all manner of drivers and teams including Team HARD, Rebecca Jackson (aka Rebecca Racer) and my own team, Turn Eight Racing.

It was in these roles that I realised my strengths lay in wonderful, out-of-the-box ideas that excited sponsors and drivers alike.

Even when running Turn Eight Racing in the BRSCC Porsche Championship for one exciting year, I decided I wasn't going to follow what other racers were doing at that level. For our final race of the season we partnered with a hospitality company to provide an amazing spread for our guests, complete with branded beanies and goody bags.

We were consistently told how professional we came across with our beautiful blue and pink Porsche, matching teamwear and general attitude. I was lucky to work with two highly-professional and talented drivers, as well as a small team of helpers and mechanics, which made everything so much easier. We also won a load of trophies, which was nice.

After Turn Eight, I spent most of my time writing about motorsport, road trips and electric cars, but I was stuck in a kind of limbo - I knew there was something else. I can't remember how the idea originally came about, but I was still consistently giving advice to racing drivers on how to pick up sponsorship.

I realised there was a massive need for a service that helped racing drivers think more like businesses. I wanted to create something that helped more than just the handful of drivers I was able to speak to at races.

I created Racing Mentor in December 2016 and it's not only changed my life, but I'm very proud to say that it's helped countless drivers get on track and pick up sponsorship.

I'm hoping this book will help you do that too.

If you want to say hello, ask a question or send some praise, you can reach me on jess@racingmentor.com.

PART ONE

MAKE YOURSELF DESIRABLE

In 2009, I decided to set up a fitness and fashion blog. I had no idea what would come from it, but just a few years later I was being nominated for awards, was named as one of the most influential fashionistas on Twitter by The Telegraph and had more free clothes and shoes than I knew what to do with. Cool, right?

I then did the same with an automotive blog, then with my profile as a journalist. I might not be a natural salesperson, but I know how to build a profile.

This is so important in motorsport too.

I had people coming to me offering me money to talk about them to my audience. It seemed like a stupidly simple way to make money and I was easily reeling in four figures every month just with blog posts.

What I did in 2009 with that blog is very similar to what you need to do as a racing driver in order to pick up ongoing sponsorship that keeps you climbing the motorsport ladder.

1.

Motorsport Sponsorship has Changed

Just like many other industries, motorsport has evolved over the years - from the way fans interact with the sport through to how businesses are leveraging it for marketing purposes.

As a racing driver, you need to understand why businesses put money into motorsport and what they want to get from it.

Unfortunately for you, business owners and marketing departments are a lot less keen to plough money into a driver in exchange for a sticker. While some people still want the prestige of being involved with the sport, most of the ones you pitch to will want something more tangible in return for their money.

Businesses need real-world results - and what that means depends on what you race in, who you're working with and what you've agreed - but, typically, businesses want to work with drivers who have highly-engaged audiences that can bring in sales and brand awareness.

Back in the early days of motorsport sponsorship, the advertising value of a sticker on a prestigious race car was usually enough to give a business return on investment. These days, we're so over-exposed to advertising that it barely registers.

Now, you'll see racing drivers acting as models, ambassadors, after-dinner speakers, sales people and so much more.

You've probably seen Lewis Hamilton walking the catwalk, Matt Neal posing with car parts or Mark Webber speaking at events - while all these drivers race at the top end of motorsport, no matter where you are in your journey there's a lot you can learn from them.

The thing these drivers - and successful ones a little lower down the motorsport ladder - have in common is reach. They have an audience, and whether that audience is online, following them around or at the track, they have something very valuable to offer brands.

I created this book to help you think beyond the limits of a sticker on a car. If you can become more than a racing driver by growing your audience and offering, you're going to be able to attract more sponsors.

Slow down

This book is split into **six parts** and, while I'm sure you're itching to get to the section about writing a pitch email, hold fire just for now.

In order to send a winning pitch, you need to offer something impressive. The first half of this book will help you to build an audience, get your name out there and establish exactly what benefits you can offer to a business.

Even if you already have an impressive audience, read on. The rest of this section goes into detail about leveraging different social networks, building a name for yourself in the press and using a blog to establish your expertise.

All of this is so important to building your personal brand and using it to attract high-value sponsorship.

Why Build an Audience Online?

You need to build an audience before you start because, if you don't, what do you really have to offer to sponsors?

You should think of yourself as a product and it's your job to sell that product to businesses. If your product only has one feature (a sticker on a race car), you aren't going to get very far. You need to be multi-faceted and people need to be listening to you.

It's possible to seek sponsorship while building an audience and some sponsors can even help with audience growth - but, if you're looking for big bucks, your audience needs to be established first.

The easiest way to get the ball rolling is online. These next few chapters will include the basics of building an audience across social media and other online platforms. Your social followings will make up some of the most important numbers that you'll be presenting to a business.

Businesses pay for followers. You'll no doubt have seen Instagram stars promoting really random products; they get paid for this. It's usually a set rate per 1,000 or 10,000 followers from a specialist agency but it's something you, as a racing driver with a niche audience, can replicate.

Content is key

Before you read on to how you build your audience across these different platforms, remember that content is key. If you're consistently posting great content (text, images and videos), your follower numbers are going to grow organically.

Experiment with different post types and regularities to work out what's best for your audience.

2.

Leveraging Facebook

The typical audience on a Facebook profile tends to be friends and family and, while this is a great place to start, you need to cast your net a little wider. First and foremost, you should be updating on a regular basis to test the waters, because if you can't get your family and friends to root for you, you've got no hope.

Once these people are engaged, consider adding people you know from motorsport. No one will understand the ins and outs of your racing life better than other racers - plus, Facebook can be a great networking tool.

You should also consider a Facebook page. While you might not always be able to get the same levels of engagement on a page compared to your personal profile, it lends a level of professionalism to your work as a racing driver.

But don't let it fall by the wayside - update regularly and, even when you can't think of something to talk about, post a picture of your race car. Everyone loves a race car.

Your page is going to be populated by friends and family to begin with, and that's fine, because the more content you post that's relevant and interesting, the further those people will help it to spread.

As you make more friends on Facebook, invite them to like your page but don't take it personally if they choose not to.

What you post on your profile can be a little more casual and colloquial, whereas your page is what fans and potential sponsors will see. I'm not saying you should suck all the personality out of it, but you should certainly be a little more professional and put more thought into how the posts will help you achieve your goals.

Post Examples:

On your personal profile:

Wow. What a great race! It was great to see so many people there and I can't believe my cousins from Australia were able to make it. Thank you for your support. We start third in the next race. I'm totally chasing another podium.

On your page:

Race one was fantastic. Thank you to my team for giving me such a wonderful car. It was great to have my family watching alongside the team from [sponsor's name]. We start third in the next race so I'm hoping for my second podium of the weekend.

You see, there's not that much difference between these two posts but they serve very different purposes. Your profile is there to update friends and family, while your page is a place for you to promote yourself, team and sponsors.

Get in front of the camera

As with most social channels, video is key. If you can record honest, fun videos for your audience, you're going to get far more engagement than if you only post some words with an image.

People want to see *YOU*.

Think about all the bloggers and influencers out there. Their pages are filled with videos of them updating their fans about all sorts of things: life, love, business, general banality, products they love, etc.

Take time to go through the Facebook pages of high-level racers and bloggers you know, and admire. Look at their content to see what gets engagement and what's working for them. From here, you can start to brainstorm ways to build your followings and encourage people to engage on Facebook using images, text posts and video.

Looking at reach

If you already have a Facebook page, you may have noticed that each post tells you exactly how many people it's reached. Keep an eye on this - not only is it useful information when pitching to potential sponsors, but it gives you a baseline to work from.

I've been using Facebook as a marketing tool for almost 10 years, and in that time the algorithms that serve your posts to your audience have changed as much as the look of the social network. First and foremost, there's a lot of value placed on engagement, so the more people who like and comment on your post just after it's been published, the further it'll reach.

Facebook also places a lot of value on media, so posts with images and videos are going to do much better than a text post. This is why it's important to include an image, even if you're posting a simple update from your race weekend.

As you can imagine, Facebook also wants to keep people on its site, so posts with embedded links don't always reach as far as we might want them to. It's worth experimenting with these kinds of links (the ones that show an image and preview from the site you're linking to) alongside image posts with a link in the text of your message.

Finally, if you want your post to reach far and wide, you need to encourage sharing as well as comments and likes. If your friends are sharing your posts to their profiles, great! But you should also share your own posts into relevant Facebook groups.

For those of you who are a little time-poor, use Facebook's scheduling tool to batch-create a number of posts to go out when you're likely to receive the most engagement (e.g. not when you're just about to get up at 5am on a Friday ready to travel to a race). You could also use a third party tool such as Buffer to schedule posts across multiple social accounts.

Facebook Groups

For the type of business I'm in, a Facebook group has been invaluable. The Racing Mentor Sponsorship Community is the place where I can run ideas past my most loyal followers; it's a group where they feel safe to share advice, as well as ask for it, and we're all rallying for one another to do well.

Not only that but, due to the way in which Facebook's algorithm works, you're more likely to see content from groups you're part of. By setting up a group, there's a greater likelihood of reaching the people who want to see your content.

Later in this book we touch on finding a niche for yourself. Once you've been through that process and you're starting to feel like more than a racing driver, it might be time to think about your own group.

To ease yourself in, you might start talking about your racing and other interests on relevant groups. Remember to not be salesy. Create content that people want to read and start to build that trust.

When the time comes to create your own group, you need to think about what people want to talk about and how a group could benefit your existing audience.

For example you might:

- » Start a fitness group for racing drivers
- » Share some performance driving trips in your own group
- » Start a support group for racing drivers with mental health issues

---

Find your niche and own it while delivering value to the people who are reading your content.

Again, this is a great way of building an engaged audience that will impress sponsors further down the line.

A note on asking for sponsorship on social media

One of my more controversial blog posts on the Racing Mentor website called out racing drivers for begging for money on social media.

These posts aren't exactly few and far between, some are good and actively talk about the benefits to these sponsors while others go on about the driver's career so far and how they need help to get to the next level.

I find this really frustrating because there are drivers out there with great reach, going into high flying series who are going to struggle to get anywhere with this kind of approach.

People don't care that you need support. They don't care about your struggles. In some rare cases you might get some money from a distant uncle who has taken pity on you but you're not going to land a £50,000 deal by posting on Facebook.

I know that this practice isn't going to stop so if you're desperate to post on social media about your search for sponsorship, here's how to do it right:

Want to boost your business and get involved in grassroots motorsport? I have opportunities available for passionate businesses looking to tap into a network of motorsport enthusiasts, increase conversions and put their brand name in front of thousands.

[Insert a line about you and what you're racing here]

Get in touch for further details.

Or, if you have impressive stats, try this:

If you're looking for new ways to market your brand this year, a partnership within motorsport can increase brand visibility and help to build an enviable social following. I can connect you with a loyal audience who trust my opinion on all things automotive. Across my social channels I have a combined following of 30,000, as well as 2,000 email subscribers.

This year I am running in [race series] and hope to add to my list of wins and podiums. Any partners coming on board will benefit from a dedicated brand ambassador who can help convert social follows into sales, VIP hospitality at races – which present plenty of opportunities to reach new clients – television coverage reaching approximately 25,000 people per day and much more.

Get in touch if you'd like to discuss over coffee, my treat.

Leave something for your prospects to find out over that coffee. Once you're further through this book and have built your social followings, you'll have more of an idea of what you can offer and the benefits you can bring to a business.

3.

Twitter

Not just a place for people to talk about what they had for breakfast or rant about the weather, Twitter is actually a brilliant marketing tool. Unlike Facebook, you can engage with people who don't follow you, you can reach new people with interesting hashtags and you can build a rapport with potential sponsors.

Before you start using Twitter to find sponsorship leads, you need to build your following. The easiest way to do this is by posting interesting and engaging content with relevant hashtags, whilst also replying to other people's Tweets.

Don't feel you need to follow thousands of people, or unfollow those that don't follow back - start small and build an audience around your content. The one thing more valuable than big follower numbers is engagement, so don't buy followers and don't use underhanded tricks to get people to follow you.

Create something wonderful and those people will naturally come to you. This is the kind of audience that sponsors want to pay for.

Once again, media content works really well on Twitter as photos and videos take up a larger space in someone's feed. Being able to grab their attention in this way is important, as it leads to increased engagement.

The odd text-only post is fine but, if you have a relevant image to go with an update, post it. You should also post your video content to Twitter as well as other social networks. It can be a good place to showcase what you're doing and point people in the direction of more video content on Facebook or YouTube.

If you feel you don't have the time to post to Twitter regularly, you can schedule posts using a platform such as Buffer. This means you can post when your audience is most active, rather than only when you have the time.

Your bio

'Racing driver looking for support for next season' isn't going to excite anyone. In fact, it's probably going to make people scroll past.

Think long and hard about your bio and what you think people will be interested in. Of course, mention that you're a racing driver, but remember - you are more than that.

Let's look at some example bios to see what works:

British Touring Car Driver and independent champion 2010&2017, Ambassador for Spine, BRDC Member.

This is straight-to-the-point, states exactly who the driver is and shows their success.

Driver for @bigteam. Chasing dreams! In partnership with @sponsor and @anothersponsor. Follow on Facebook & Instagram @XX

There are lots of mentions in this bio, which makes it easy for people to click through and follow other accounts. This is a great way to give your sponsors some love, especially if you're picking up a lot of new followers from your activity.

> Racing driver and personal trainer competing in @series. Writing about human performance in motorsport @blog. Sponsored by @fitnesscompany and @biggym.

This is a good example of a driver who has found their niche. This is going to attract the attention of fitness buffs as well as those interested in motorsport and cars.

Pinned tweet

When people visit your profile to try and work out if they want to follow you back, they'll have a look at your first few tweets. Make sure your pinned tweet is indicative of the kind of content you'll be posting.

For me, I tend to pin general things around sponsorship or motorsport careers. This gives anyone who pops along to my profile an idea of what I do.

As a racing driver, you should be pinning photos of you on the podium, a run-down of your latest racing activity, a video you've created for a sponsor or even a vlog where you introduce yourself. Try to go beyond what your bio says and give people a reason to follow you.

Hashtags

Using relevant hashtags in your posts allows the people following those tags or browsing through them to find your tweet, even if they're not following you directly.

> The tags you use depend on what you're talking about but many race series have their own hashtags, so make sure to use them.

The **#F1, #BTCC, #VASC, #FormulaE, #WeareGinetta** and **#WEC** hashtags tend to reach quite far, so be sure to use them if you're talking about those series.

You can also use **#motorsport**, but you probably need to be a bit more specific if you're going to reach the right people. Look for hashtags relevant to the make of your race car, the circuit you're at, your home town and so on.

Once you start posting more business-orientated content, the tags **#SMEs, #smallbi**z and **#biz** all tend to work well and can often pick you up a few more followers.

One thing to remember, though, is that more isn't necessarily better. Restrain yourself from using multiple hashtags in one post; studies have shown that tweets with just one or two hashtags get far more engagement than those with loads. In fact, a wall of hashtags can look spammy, causing people to just scroll past your post without reading.

Following people you want to hear from

Follow people and businesses you're interested in - some of them might follow you back, some won't. Don't take it personally, just as you shouldn't feel bad if you choose not to follow someone back yourself.

There's a horrible practice across social media of following and unfollowing people in order to grow your own follower count whilst keeping the following number low. This makes people look more popular than they probably are.

While those inflated figures might look good on the surface, they actually serve very little purpose. Businesses are just as interested in engagement rates as they are in follower counts.

Many businesses would rather work with a highly-engaged audience of 50% out of 1,000 than they would 5% out of 10,000.

Getting people to follow you back

If someone doesn't follow you back, it might be because they're not sure if they'll be interested in what you've got to say. This is the reason you need to keep your bio and pinned tweet interesting and up-to-date (if in doubt, ask for frank feedback from friends, family and fellow racers on their first impressions of your profile).

The other way to get people to follow back is to engage with them. As you're following them, they'll start to appear in your timeline so, if you see an interesting tweet, get involved in the conversation.

This doesn't have to take a lot of time out of your day or week, but spend some time scrolling through your timeline (while the kettle boils, for example) and reply whenever you have something interesting or valuable to say.

Not only does this expose your account to more people, but the person you're replying to might give you a follow back when they realise you've got something interesting to say.

Get involved in big conversations

As well as replying to the people you follow, you should get involved in other conversations. If a tweet about motorsport or something else you're interested in has gone viral with hundreds of replies, get involved. By replying to one of these threads, you're exposing yourself and your account to a huge amount of people.

Make sure you have something interesting and relevant (or witty) to say. Bonus points if it links to what you do as a racing driver and you can naturally relate it back to your experiences.

Too many people see Twitter as a one-sided thing, that if they post they'll suddenly have thousands of followers. Unfortunately, it's not that simple, and Twitter is something you need to work at. But, once you do build a decent following, it's a valuable tool.

4.

YouTube

I'm going to start with a stat that should show you just how valuable YouTube is:

81% of businesses use video marketing

I could go into detail on the stats because I'm a nerd, but this is the only one that's really relevant to you at this stage. Big businesses are using video to make sales, understand their customer base and inform people.

If you can approach businesses offering your own YouTube channel as a platform for their video marketing material, you're onto a winner.

Again, YouTube is about great content. Make videos that people want to see and, while it's OK to create content that you know works (vlogs, for example), think outside the box. You're in a very crowded market so you need to stand out.

Later in this book, we'll touch on the types of videos you can create to promote sponsors, which is a good starting point for brainstorming content that will help you to grow your subscriber count.

Cross-promote

The best way to grow your YouTube channel is to cross-promote it on your other channels, especially if you've already successfully grown your audience elsewhere.

Make sure you're posting your videos to Facebook, Twitter and LinkedIn - you could even tease the release of a video on your Instagram or Facebook stories.

Look at what YouTubers outside of motorsport are doing to engage with their audiences.

Use cards

Using cards and YouTube's other built-in marketing tools can help you cross-promote your videos and encourage people to subscribe. Don't be afraid to experiment with these tools to increase views and follower numbers.

At the very least, you should have a card at the end of your video that encourages people to subscribe.

Healthy video views and a good subscriber count are important, so you'll want to do everything you can to encourage people to stick around after they've watched one video.

Get your thumbnail right

The thumbnail of your video is one of the elements that will draw a person in and get them to click. You can set a custom thumbnail when you upload your video, so make sure you have something with a little bit of text that tells people exactly what the video is about.

It's also good to use a professionally-shot photo or a non-blurry still from the video. Make it look as sharp as possible - you need to stand out amongst the vast number of in-car footage and poorly-shot race weekend videos out there.

5.

LinkedIn

L inkedIn is a powerful networking tool and, while it might not always give you an audience you can market to, it can help you reach the right people when you need something.

Start by making sure your profile is up-to-date and focuses on your racing career, but don't be afraid to add in notable achievements and work experience from your day job.

Pay special attention to your tag line as people will see this when you post and comment. It gives business owners a sense of who you are. Opt for something simple and to-the-point. Even for someone like me with a lot of job roles, I keep it simple: PR, journalist and motorsport consultant.

Here are some examples for racers:

>> Brand ambassador and racing driver

>> After-dinner speaker and motorcycle racer

>> Brand ambassador for [big brand]

>> Marketing consultant who races cars

>> Racing driver and influencer

You should also be connecting with anyone you can who is relevant. That includes other racing drivers, motorsport professionals, engineers, HR people, CEOs, local businesses, friends and family.

Once you have some connections, keep an eye on your LinkedIn feed and comment on interesting posts. This is the first step in getting your name out there as it'll show up, along with your tag line, when others look through the post and the discussion surrounding it.

You should also be posting. What you'd post on your Facebook page is just as relevant for LinkedIn, but don't be afraid to start discussions, too. Ask people for their opinion on races, motorsport news and anything else you're interested in.

If you're already active on LinkedIn as part of your day job or own business, you can still leverage this audience. Firstly, you'll already have connections who could be potential sponsors so it's important to engage with them so they know who you are when you're ready to pitch.

Even if you want to keep your LinkedIn dedicated to you day job, there's nothing wrong with mentioning your racing career and interest in motorsport. We are all real people who do more than just go to work. Not only are you exposing people to your racing career in order to help it, but having a cool hobby could help you in your LinkedIn efforts related to your day job, too.

Reading the tenth post of the day about someone's recruitment process can be a little dull, whereas seeing a race car is always exciting, no matter what industry you're in.

Engagement

On all social platforms, engagement is key. Make sure you're getting excited about other people's achievements. Like, comment and message people on a regular basis and do it with no agenda.

The more you can engage with these people, the easier it'll be to turn to them when you need sponsorship. Not only will they be more receptive to your approach, but you'll have a better sense of their business and how you can help them.

Periodically go through your connections and see who you can engage with further in a private message. Remember, this first contact should have no other goal than to open the lines of communication and build a rapport. Say you're interested in what they do and would love to hear more; congratulate them on a promotion; ask a question about their business; ask for a tiny bit of advice.

Taking the time to do this now will help you in the future. It'll also make these people more receptive to your posts, encouraging them to comment and like, which is great for your post reach.

Making an approach

People on LinkedIn are getting approached every day by someone trying to sell something - I have to say, I do often ignore these people, especially those who connect and then launch straight into a sales pitch.

Your approach should be more considered. You should have spoken to the person previously and engaged with their posts. You should also understand how a partnership can benefit them specifically rather than generally (we'll go into more detail on this in later chapters).

You can pitch via LinkedIn message, but make sure the person you're contacting is active on the platform - otherwise, you might not get a reply.

It's also possible to find the email address of your target connection by going to their profile and clicking on the contact details section.

Like Twitter, LinkedIn may take some time to get right but it can prove very lucrative in the future. One of the biggest deals

I made on LinkedIn was from a single message that netted me £21,000, so don't underestimate it.

6.

Instagram

Instagram is an important brand awareness tool for you and for your sponsors. It's a great place to showcase what you can do and tends to work really well for drivers who communicate with images and video rather than words. It's also a good platform for giving an insight into your daily life.

> You should absolutely utilise the story feature on Instagram, too, as it's a great way to encourage engagement and allow people to get to know you.

Relevant images

While it's fine to post the odd selfie or pretty landscape, make sure it's relevant to your brand and your racing. With every picture you post, think about what it says about you and what you can offer to sponsors.

Hashtags

The correct use of hashtags will allow your pictures to reach far and wide. A good practice is to post a collection of these in the first comment under your post - if you're struggling to find relevant hashtags, use Hashme, an app that allows you put in one relevant keyword and get a list of related ones.

Stories

These work in much the same way that Snapchat or Facebook stories do; they're time-limited posts that usually revolve around an event. For racing drivers, you should use stories (across all platforms, if you have the time) to document your race weekends, sponsor events and more.

When it comes to stats, it's easy to see how many people have viewed your story. Keep an eye on this as it's something you can sell to potential sponsors that are looking to grow their Instagram following.

Once you've reached a follower count of 10,000 (minimum for influencer status, I'd say), you'll also be able to add links to your stories. This is helpful, because you'll be able to directly link to other videos and blog posts, as well as to sponsor websites.

Engagement

Take some time to like and comment on other photos. This will help you to reach a wider audience while growing your own. Again, numbers are important and there are businesses out there which would pay a racing driver for a large Instagram audience before you even get onto all the other things you can offer.

7.

Blogging

You've no doubt heard of people who have found fame and fortune as bloggers. These influencers often get invitations to the front row of fashion shows, guest drives in race cars, paid travel to amazing places and all sorts of other perks.

Many wouldn't be able to do this without a blog alongside their popular social accounts. What you blog about is up to you, but try to be different. Everyone is talking about their race weekends so try to add something unique into your writing.

Consider finding a niche for yourself. You could talk about the technical aspects of a car build, travelling around the UK and Europe to races, getting race fit, how your kids are getting involved with the race car or something else that interests you.

There are other ways to show your expertise online - which we'll touch on in the PR section - but start with a blog and social media while encouraging people to engage with your content.

SEO value

Your blog could also work as a valuable search engine optimisation (SEO) tool for businesses. I've had a fitness and fashion blog for almost 10 years and an automotive one for about six - both of them have good, regular traffic and high Domain Authority (DA).

It's the DA that regularly has businesses banging on my door (figuratively) looking to jump on that bandwagon. If you can build something similar through your blog and website, you have something to offer potential sponsors who focus heavily on content marketing, SEO and backlinks.

You can find out your current DA at Moz.com.

Anything over 20 is good, over 30 is really valuable and over 40 will probably have businesses coming to you with minimal effort.

One great source of income for me has been responding to blogger opportunities on Facebook and Twitter. There are a number of Facebook groups and Twitter hashtags that regularly post paid work for bloggers - these are from businesses willing to pay you to write a post with a link back to their website.

Take a look at Racingmentor.com/SEO for other ways in which you can maximise this element of your offering.

8.

Calculating Your
Social Reach

Looking at your follower counts is easy, but another number you need to know about is your reach - this is the amount of people who could potentially read your posts. How you reach new people depends on the platform you're using but it could be through any combination of hashtags, shares, comments and likes.

Generally, your posts will reach more people if you get more engagement, which is why it's important to ask questions and encourage people to comment.

With each platform, experiment with reaching new people as this will give you an idea of what works best for your audience.

Facebook

Under each of your Facebook page posts, you'll see their reach, but your page also has a tab labelled 'insights' - this is where you'll find growth, reach, engagement and more.

Use these tools to get an idea of your total reach as well as per post.

Twitter

Twitter doesn't make a big deal about its powerful analytics tool, but it's there, and you should be using it to see which of your posts are reaching the most people, your engagement levels, impressions, link clicks and more.

LinkedIn

This platform will show the reach of each of your posts underneath. It's a really great way to see the impact of each post and what's working.

YouTube

Your videos will also have obvious stats in terms of views, but you can get more insights in your Creator Studio under analytics.

For other social accounts, check the built-in analytics but also consider signing up for a more detailed analytics dashboard, such as Sprout Social (paid) or Buffer (free with paid plans).

On the Blog

For your blog, most platforms come with built-in analytics but, if you need something more powerful, install Google Analytics.

Interesting statistics to look at are the amount of individual users looking at your website and the pages they're visiting. You can also look at how long each person stays on your site - the longer someone sticks around, the better, as it means they're taking time to read your content.

Find the total

Calculate your total reach by adding up the reach figures from all your social accounts.

While a lot of sponsors will want an individual breakdown of each account and how it might work for them, you can hook them with one big number - 20,000 followers with a reach of 100,000 looks much more impressive than a list of 10 accounts with smaller followings.

For more information on calculating your social reach and for all the relevant links, visit Racingmentor.com/socialreach.

9.

Engaging with Your Audience at the Track

I keep banging on about this but, while large follower numbers can look impressive, engagement is much more important. What's the point in having 50,000 followers if none of them are paying attention to your content?

It's much more valuable to have an engaged audience - and one way to ensure that is at the track.

Events

Scheduled events during a race weekend are a great way to bring people to you. You know what it's like when you see a small crowd gathering in the paddock - you want to know what's going on. By encouraging people to your garage or awning, you're likely to draw a larger crowd.

The events could be as simple as Q&As, signings and photo opportunities with you and your car, or they could be something more unique. Experiment with different ideas to see what brings people to you. At the very least, you should be engaging with your friends and family at the race track, as well as other drivers.

Flyers and banners are a good way to announce what you're doing, but your social channels (including an official Facebook event) can encourage more people - who usually follow online - to join you.

Competitions

A competition is another good way to get people to come to you during a race weekend. The easiest way to do this is by encouraging people to take a photo of your car and post it online with a certain hashtag.

You could invest in an Instagram frame for people to pose with or you could simply have a banner with the details of your competition. What you give away is up to you, but consider race weekend tickets, hospitality spots or passenger laps during a track day.

By asking people to tag you and use a certain hashtag when they post a photo, you'll increase your reach, pick up new followers and will see a lot of people sharing the excitement from the race track with their friends online.

The importance of video and photography

When thinking about attracting sponsors, you need to show them just how much engagement you could bring them. You also need to show them the kind of content you produce. Videos and images play a huge part in all of this.

Make sure to take photos of the people looking at your car, taking part in competitions or enjoying your hospitality.

It's all well and good telling a potential sponsor that you get big crowds at races but, if you can really show them the level of interest you attract, your pitch is going to have so much more power.

You should use video content to document your race weekend, but also show sponsors how you can do something similar for them.

To stand out, you need to go above and beyond - do more than what other drivers are doing.

Getting people from the safe world of the internet to the track

If you have thousands of followers online, well done - but you need to get those people to the track. Special events can be a good way to do this, but you'll need to give them an incentive.

Lay on a special hospitality spread for important followers, offer free paddock passes or hold competitions. If you can regularly draw a crowd to races, the space on your car is going to be even more valuable.

How you can involve sponsors

Once you have sponsors on board, you can get them involved in track-side events. They could offer competition prizes, you could ask people to tag them in photos or they could provide food, drinks or freebies for your guests.

This is something to discuss with your sponsors once they get on board, but I've listed a whole host of ways to involve sponsors with events later in this book.

10.

Public Relations:
Your Most Valuable Tool

The Chartered Institute of Public Relations defines PR like so:

"Public Relations is about reputation - the result of what you do, what you say and what others say about you.

"Public Relations is the discipline which looks after reputation, with the aim of earning understanding and support and influencing opinion and behaviour. It is the planned and sustained effort to establish and maintain goodwill and mutual understanding between an organisation and its public."

How you manage your reputation can happen in a number of ways, from how you present yourself at the track through to how you talk about yourself and sponsors on social media. While we've touched on some of those elements already, press coverage will be the focus of this section, as this is one of the largest elements of PR and the hardest to get right.

Press coverage can be as simple as getting your race wins printed in the local newspaper, or it could be as in-depth as a detailed documentary on your racing career.

Press coverage includes anything in newspapers, magazines, online, on the radio or on television. Some outlets will have more reach and relevance than others, but all coverage is worth something when it comes to building your audience and getting your brand beyond motorsport. This is all key when it comes to landing sponsors.

What you should be doing after each race

In order to maximise the amount of press coverage you can get from a race, you need to do a few things. The first is to write up a race report - detail the ups and downs of your race weekend, mention sponsors where you can and talk about any other activities (events, hospitality, filming and competitions) you had going on during the weekend.

You also need to consider your hook. Unfortunately, it's not enough to go to a publication with a simple race report. Sometimes your hook is easy - *'local racing driver wins international race'*. Sometimes it'll be a bit more obscure - *'vegan racing driver wins fifth race in a row'*.

Think about how you can stand out over other racing drivers who have had similar results.

Your race report will also need an image. If you've had a photographer taking photos of you during the weekend, make sure to get hi-res versions of these. When arranging photography services, make sure your chosen photographer can get images to you on the Monday ready to be sent out to press.

Your race report and photo will form the basis of a press release that can go out to press, sponsors and onto your blog.

The Purpose of a Press Release

A press release gives all the important details of a news story to a journalist. Some might lift the copy straight from it, others might use it to inform their own writing. Either way, it needs to be well-written and informative.

The first paragraph is the most important - make sure you include all the main points in your opener so a journalist can instantly get the gist of the story. Follow the rule of who, what, when, why, where and how.

Advice from the press

Jack Phillips, digital editor at Motor Sports Magazine, has this advice for racing drivers looking to impress with a press release:

"What I really look for in a press release is a real person and a sense of character. That's how you're more likely to pick up our interest.

"Similarly, stock quotes and soundbites – 'looking to bounce back' or 'aiming for the top step' and such like – really serve no purpose because we're never going to run those. Genuine insights or honesty is far more interesting.

"There should also be no expectation of sites, particularly one like ours, to run them when there's no story. An understanding of that will help in the long run; it's about pitching something that is of genuine interest to a journalist. A driver going racing to win isn't interesting - a driver actually doing something out of the norm is. It's about packaging it and being realistic."

How to contact the press

In an ideal world, you'll have had a chance to build a rapport with a journalist (on social media or at the track, for example) before you pitch to them, but I know that's not always possible.

To find journalist contacts, all you need to do is look for the masthead in a magazine - this is the section of the magazine that gives contact details for the publisher and says who contributed articles.

Sometimes you'll find a specific email address for the editor; other times you'll have to do a little more digging by visiting the publisher's website or making a phone call.

For other outlets, a call is usually the best way to find the information you need. Often you'll just get the newsdesk email, which is a general email that will be picked up by someone in the newsroom. This is a great place to start but, if you can get the name and email of a specific journalist dealing with the relevant section (usually sport or motoring), even better!

What your press coverage means to sponsors

Your press coverage is an indicator to sponsors that you're able to reach a wide audience. For many sponsors, getting press coverage is a huge benefit of working with a racing driver, but they're not going to trust that you can do it without seeing proof.

If you promise potential sponsors similar coverage to what you're already getting, there's huge benefit for them in terms of reaching new customers, raising brand awareness and showing off their support for a racing driver.

Working out your press reach

If you need extra ammunition to convince sponsors what a good deal they're getting by working with you, you should include your press reach and value.

First start by making a list of all the press coverage you've picked up over the last 12 months.

It might look like this:

» Checkered Flag - 3

» Local newspaper - 4
» Local website - 2
» BBC local radio - 1
» Autosport - 1
» Turn Eight - 1
» Motorsport TV - 1

To work out your reach, you need to find out the readership for all these outlets. This information can usually be found by contacting the advertising department of the magazine, newspaper, website, radio station or television channel.

A lot of the information is publicly available online - especially for bigger outlets - but for some of the smaller ones, you may need to call. For any websites you can't get in touch with or who are reluctant to give stats, you can use Similarweb.com.

Once you have all the readership stats, multiply each figure by the amount of coverage you've had during the year. For example, if your local newspaper has a readership of 20,000 and you've appeared in it four times, your reach is 80,000. (20,000 x 4 = 80,000.)

Do this for each outlet and then add all these numbers together to find your reach for the year.

Working out the value of press coverage

To work out the value of your year's coverage, you need to look at the equivalent advertising cost for similar space.

Again, you can find out this information by requesting a rate card from the publication. If you can't buy advertising with that outlet (such as the BBC), the value of your coverage is literally priceless.

So, let's say your coverage in the local paper was around half a page, and to buy a half-page ad would cost £250. With four pieces of coverage, that's a value of £1,000. (250 x 4 = 1,000.)

Do this for all pieces of coverage and add up the total. The likelihood is that the number you come away with is going to be more than you're asking for from a sponsor.

These figures are useful because it goes further than simply telling a sponsor how much you could do for them - it shows them.

Interested to find out more?

I could write an entire book on PR (maybe I will!) but have chosen to cover just the basics here. Doing your own PR is a huge time investment and often a steep learning curve.

My advice would be to start small with the local and motorsport press but, if you want to start tackling the bigger fish such as national newspapers and glossy lifestyle magazines, check out our Ultimate Guide to PR course. It's a course aimed at racing drivers of every level who are eager to learn how to do their own PR and use it to pick up sponsors.

Because you bought this book, you get 25% off too. Visit Racingmentor.com/PR for all the details.

11.

Getting Known

Getting known gives you prestige, allows you the upper hand when you introduce yourself and gives you more influence with your audience. I don't want to call this fame, because you don't necessarily have to be famous to be a well-known racing driver.

What's important is that people know who you are. Press coverage is a big part of this but growing your audience and engaging with them is important too. This section of the book will teach you how to get known in motorsport, your local area and beyond.

By becoming an influencer in these areas, businesses will be more likely to come to you looking for your influence over an audience.

Think about how bloggers and YouTube stars engage with their audiences and how hard they work to keep pushing out amazing content, while getting their faces out there at events and in the press. This is what you should be aiming for as a racing driver.

Start by thinking about the influencers you admire and look into what they're doing, how they got there and how often they're uploading new content. Even across different influence levels and niches, you'll see that these people are talking directly to their audiences and creating content for them.

Locally

Start small and focus on getting known in your local area. The easiest way to do this is through regular coverage in the local press, but you also need to get out to events. By showing your face publicly in your teamwear, and perhaps even doing vlogs, people will start to recognise you.

Don't feel under pressure to go to every event that comes up, but do make sure you're involved with your local community in some way. These people can not only turn out to be a loyal audience, but connecting with them can also be a great networking tool.

It's also important to stay active on social media. As well as updating your racing accounts with your adventures - local and otherwise - you should be getting involved in local groups, especially on Facebook.

In Motorsport

Getting known in motorsport is a little more difficult as it's such a crowded market. The key here is to be consistent with your social media and get involved in relevant groups. For example, if you're a club racer in the UK, there are a number of Facebook groups out there dedicated to British motorsport. You should also be able to find groups relevant to the make of your race car and the series you compete in.

While becoming known in motorsport is great, you generally need to be doing something very different to everyone else. Perhaps you're vlogging your car build or documenting your journey to becoming race-fit - find yourself a niche that's relevant to your interests and personality, and run with it.

What I do in the journalism world is similar. I could've focused my efforts on car reviews, just like everyone else, but I found myself two niches instead - sponsorship and the business of motorsport, as well as future car tech.

Everywhere Else

This is your key to becoming more than just a racing driver. Look at the way Lewis Hamilton gets involved in fashion and music, or how Jackie Stewart was an Olympic-level shooter.

Again, your fitness journey or car build could interest people outside of motorsport. Look to fitness press, influencers and groups as a way of getting your name out there, or start submitting car build progress to technical automotive press and websites.

Think about your interests outside of motorsport and consider how they could tie-in with your racing. Make a list of all the things you're into and brainstorm ways they could become your identifying factor in motorsport. Even if you can't find your own niche, it should help you come up with some great ideas for events and press that reach new people.

Example Brainstorm

Football

- » Charity football match with racing drivers
- » Charity kart race with footballers
- » How to fuel/condition your body for both sports

Fashion

- » Race day outfits
- » The development of your own clothing line
- » Looking closely at the design elements of different race cars and liveries

Gaming

- » From gamer to racing driver

> » How racing games match up to real life
> » Comparing real-life race cars to in-game ones
> » How first-person-shooters can improve reaction times for racing

Food

> » Race day food
> » Meal prep
> » Restaurant reviews around race tracks
> » How to eat vegan/paleo/keto/vegetarian/clean during a race weekend

Travel

> » Race circuits and karting tracks around the world
> » Best places to stay near race tracks
> » What to see when you travel to...
> » Packing for a race weekend

There's so much content you can create around your chosen niche. While you can make it relevant to your racing, don't be afraid to step out of that box for wider appeal.

One of my coaching clients was a little stuck with how to position himself. He was a business owner as well as racing driver, but didn't feel that was enough of a niche. As we went on to talk about video content, he showed me a video of his daughter commentating on one of his races.

As someone who clearly cared for his family and brought them along to each race, it made sense to nurture this. He decided to explore the parenting niche within motorsport alongside his business experience and success as a rookie.

How to use your reach

Once you have this reach into other areas, you need to understand how valuable it is. Is your audience eager to book the hotel you've recommended near Zandvoort? Are they hanging on your every word when it comes to a race-ready diet?

Think about how your audience reacts to your content and use that in your pitches. Use specific examples of how people are engaging with your content, if you can. If not, it's fine to be more general. You might mention to a health food brand that you have a reach of 100,000 (calculated from your social stats), the majority of whom are interested in your fitness and nutrition content.

Make people root for you

No matter what niche you become well known in - be it in your local area, within motorsport or beyond - you need to make people root for you.

I think this is a fine line to tread. I know racing drivers who spin everything into a positive and, while people enjoy the good news stories, it doesn't give them anything to root for. If you read a novel where the protagonist is always doing well, you'd get bored pretty quickly.

I'm not saying you should invent hardships when you're doing well, but you should be honest about your exploits. Sometimes things just don't go to plan, despite all the hard work you've put in getting ready for a race.

While it's hard to get behind an ever-positive driver, it's also difficult to cheer for someone who can never see the positives of a situation. Keep your down-in-the-dumps, woe-is-me complaining to a minimum and express it only when it's truly warranted.

This is racing - sometimes your car will break during testing. Sometimes your teammate will crash on the first lap of an endurance race. Sometimes an over-zealous youngster will make a bad overtake and put you in the wall. Sometimes, you'll get cocky and will put the championship leader into the gravel. These things happen.

You need to show people how hard you work both on and off the race track. Even if your audience has never met you, they should be consuming enough of your videos and content to feel like they know you.

12.

What you can Offer

One of the biggest parts of creating a pitch for a sponsor is understanding what you can offer. Sponsorship is about so much more than stickers on a car, and it's unlikely businesses will give you money without something in exchange.

Once you've built your reputation and you have an audience, you'll have something tangible and useful to offer a business. This is why it's so important to take time to work on your social media and PR before you even send a pitch.

Features vs Benefits

It's important to understand the difference between features and benefits:

» A **feature** is a surface statement about what you offer.
» A **benefit** is the end result for the sponsor.

For example, hospitality at a race event is a great thing you can offer to a sponsor, but you really need to spell out *why* it's an important part of a sponsorship package. It's a fantastic money-can't-buy reward for businesses to offer for customer

GET PAID TO RACE

and employee engagement. If you also have other businesses attending, it could also be a great networking opportunity.

The table below shows examples of how you might list out the benefits of what you can offer.

Feature	Benefit
Branding on a race car	Exposure to X potential new customers on television and at the circuit
Branded race car available for events	Draw potential customers to an event stand as a talking point and photo opportunity
Social media mentions	Reach X people interested in [sponsor's industry], increasing brand awareness and driving website visits
Hospitality	Offer money-can't-buy experiences to give back to staff and VIP customers, increasing employee retention and sales
Racing driver available for speaking events	Draw crowds to your events and engage them with tales from the world of racing, promoting your business and getting more people in front of your products

We'll cover how to formulate all this into a pitch to a business in later chapters but, for now, I want you to just think about what you can offer and why that might be important to a business.

Take some time to create your own table listing what you can offer and then work out how it might benefit a sponsor. Bear in mind that this could differ for each business you contact.

Your audience

You'll have already worked out your total reach from press coverage and on your social channels, but you also need to understand the kind of people who follow you. It's likely that if you've been working on creating a specific niche for yourself, you'll have people in your audience that are interested in those things. That's a good place to start.

Are the people who follow you petrol-heads, mechanics, fitness fanatics, travellers? Again, all the insights on Twitter and Facebook will give you a good sense of who your followers are, their age ranges, genders and so on. This is all valuable information to use when approaching sponsors.

It's also possible to simply ask through polls and surveys what your audience is interested in.

For your press coverage, you can find demographic information from the advertising departments of the magazines/websites you're featured in, in case you need more ammo when approaching businesses.

Anyone selling fitness gear, for example, will want to know your audience is actually interested in buying those kinds of products.

Similarly, if you have an estimated audience of 10,000 - all of whom are motorsport enthusiasts - it's probably not worth pitching for a partnership with a green energy company based on that (unless they're all Formula E fans, of course).

Why you?

As well as being able to tell sponsors all they need to know about what you offer and the kind of people you can help them reach, you need to specifically tell them why they should choose you over other racing drivers.

In a lot of cases, the fact that you've built an audience will be enough, but don't be afraid to get personal. Are you targeting that particular travel company because you met the love of your life on one of its trips? Maybe you're targeting a health brand because it changed your life. You don't always have to have a personal story to go with your pitch but, if you do, it's going to have even more impact.

Why does anyone need this?

Again, you need to think about why anyone would sponsor you. Put yourself in a business owner's shoes and consider why sponsoring a driver would make sense from their perspective.

At every step of crafting your pitch and working out what you can offer, ask yourself, "why does anyone need this?"

PART TWO

DEFINING YOUR OFFERING

As I've said before, many drivers tend to think that a sticker on a car and a seat in hospitality is enough to convince a huge sponsor to come on board - but that's not the case.

This section touches on all the things you could offer a business, why they're relevant and how you can relate them to a business's goals (which is covered more in Part Three).

Use this part of the book as a guide to brainstorming your own offering, and don't be afraid to think outside the box.

How to brainstorm

Open a Word document, create new Google Doc or pick up a pen and paper. As you go through this section of the book, write down what you could offer then start to expand each point.

Ask yourself these questions:

- » How would your offering benefit a business?
- » What do you need to make it happen?
- » Who could help you?

- » How much would it cost?
- » What challenges might you face offering this to sponsors?
- » How can you overcome them?

With each thing you can or want to offer, consider the logistics and costs of each, as this will determine how much you should charge sponsors for access to that part of your sponsorship package.

This list isn't exhaustive; it's designed to spark ideas. Don't limit yourself to what everyone else is doing.

13.

Thinking Outside the Box

When planning this book, I needed to think outside the box because traditional publishing is a pain in the butt. I knew if I went down that route it'd be a long process with either no advance or, at best, a minimal one (an advance is the money you get to cover the writing of the book. For celebrities writing a tell-all biography, it'd be in the tens of thousands, maybe more. For me, the best case scenario would've been about £500).

So, I thought outside of the box following a wonderful suggestion from someone in the Racing Mentor Sponsorship group on Facebook, and began to seek out sponsorship for the very book you're reading right now.

I got paid to write this book and self-publish it, which meant it got into your hands very quickly - plus I get to keep a larger chunk of my royalties. It's win-win for everyone.

There have been a few other instances of people seeking sponsorship for a book so I was hardly alone but, in the motorsport world, people jumped at the idea. Not only was it wonderful to see the support coming in for the book, but I get to work with some amazing companies promoting their products and services.

I, of course, offered more than a logo on the book cover and those of you who follow me on social media, have watched my videos and read my blog will see these sponsors popping up all over the place.

The following chapters are a guide based on my own experiences in motorsport, marketing and PR. Use them directly, if you like, but don't be afraid to come up with wacky, out-of-this-world ideas to promote your sponsors.

When Jess thinks outside the box

These are all real ideas I've pitched to sponsors that have signed on the dotted line.

» Driver to host tasting of sponsor's teas with select influencers, bloggers and journalists

» Driver to take over sponsor's social media to document their morning routine (including the sponsor's coffee products)

» Quotes from driver to be sent out to the press on business/tech tips that feature sponsor products

» Driver to host a drift day teaching sponsor's key customers how to drift

» International networking events hosted by driver at different races around the world to promote the sponsor and cater to its suppliers and customers

» Driver to host an event for competition winners where they're taught precision driving skills before competing in a timed skill test

» Sponsor to provide post-event hospitality to reach driver's guests with talks, drinks and nibbles

» Workout videos led by the driver for use on the sponsor's website and social channels

---

» Public fitness events where the driver takes part and acts as a brand ambassador for the sponsor

14.

Branding

Let's start with what you know: stickers! I'm quite critical of people who offer nothing but stickers to brand because, when used alone, branding on a race car just doesn't work as an advertising tool. That being said, having a logo on a race car can add all sorts of other benefits to a brand. Firstly, it's really cool and, for some petrol-head business owners, that's a motivating factor when it comes to sponsoring a race car.

Beyond the cool points, a logo on a car, your race suit or your merch can boost a brand's profile if the company in question is willing to get involved in marketing the partnership. If they're not, it's down to you to get people in front of that logo through events, social media and press coverage.

A Sticker on Your Car

When you offer a sticker on your car to a sponsor, you need to let them know how it should be used. It doesn't really work as an advertising tool because there are stickers on every single car out there, and normal punters tend to just look past them. This is called 'advertising blindness' and it happens everywhere, which is why businesses are becoming more savvy to influencer marketing and other out-of-the-box techniques.

Instead, branding on a race car should be offered as a way to promote a brand away from the race track. It's a powerful tool to use on social media, at events and on the company website.

Logo on Your Race Suit or Helmet

This can be more powerful than branding on a car because, when you're on screen or talking to people in person, you're not swamped by logos so one or two are able to stand out. If you win a race and get interviewed on television, then those logos are going to have pride of place. The same goes for paddock photography, portraits and your photo in the paper.

A sponsor logo on your race helmet, a cap you wear on the podium and on your teamwear also serve the same purpose.

Branding on Your Merch

If you offer merchandise to your fans, sponsors, friends and family, give your partners the chance to be part of that. Everyone loves to walk around in quality clothing with their logo on so make sure to offer this as part of any sponsor package.

Not only is it a nice perk, but those logos will be seen beyond the race track.

Logos on Your Website

Be sure to offer logos on your website and social channels. This is a chance for sponsors to reach more people and be involved in your wider racing brand. If you include a link back to a sponsor's website, it can also have important SEO value.

It's also good for you to show off the support you get from reputable businesses.

While it's important to think of branding as a key part of a sponsorship package, it shouldn't be the only thing you offer. Most business owners will see it as a given and won't want to know *if* you're offering branding, they'll want to know where and how many people it'll reach.

15.

Social Media

Your social media presence is so important because it gives you a chance to reach millions of people globally, even if you only race in your local area.

If you can build an impressive following and a strong brand, there's so much you can offer your sponsors. If you haven't already done this, go back to the first section of this book where I talk about building an audience online.

Regular social posts

You can offer social posts as part of any sponsorship package. This can help your sponsor reach a new audience, build its followings and increase enquiries. Once again, it's good for the brand to be associated with a racing driver.

The number of posts depends on your agreement with the sponsor, but consider how your audience will react to multiple posts simply telling them to follow that sponsor.

Your social posts still need to serve your audience so, instead of just name-dropping your sponsor as part of a contractual obligation, consider posting the helpful driving tips that appeared on its website, some images from one of its events or a video review of one of its products.

Your other activity for the sponsor can feed your social media and make it much more natural than a forced post because you signed a contract.

Social media Q&A

A social media Q&A on your sponsor's channels boosts engagement and generates interest in what the business is doing in motorsport. This obviously works best if you have a large, loyal following but there's no reason it couldn't work if you haven't yet built this audience. Be aware, however, that if you organise this and you don't get many questions, it's going to reflect badly on you. It's always a good tactic to ask friends and family to get the ball rolling with the first few questions.

Social media takeover

Another option is to offer to take over the sponsor's social media for a day. This works well using Instagram in particular, where you could post images and videos from a race weekend both as standard posts and as part of a story. It gives the company lots of new content for future use but it'll also bring in new followers and lots of engagement.

It works well on other social channels, too, and any brands that seem to struggle with consistent posting would be glad to have someone else taking the reins.

Easy social content

Make it easy for your sponsors to post about your achievements, especially after a race weekend. Even if a sponsor is keen to support you and use your racing as a branding tool, it doesn't always happen. If you can make life easy for your sponsors, they'll thank you for it.

When you send out race reports, include a few lines and an image that can be used on social media. The text can then simply be copied and pasted into whatever social network they use and the image easily attached alongside it.

Not only are you helping your sponsors populate their social channels, but you're also helping them to promote what you're doing.

16.

Your Website

A professional website is a must if you want a presence to show off to potential sponsors. Not only that, but it can be a big draw for sponsors looking for online and SEO (search engine optimisation) benefits.

You website doesn't have to be complicated, it just has to look good. You don't need to spend thousands to get a website up to scratch - unless you want to sell merch - but you need to have a web presence that accurately reflects your brand.

Race reports

Get reports from each race on your website. It can even be a short write-up or link to an official announcement, but a regularly-updated website not only looks great and shows people you're racing, it's also good for SEO. Google likes it when you post.

You can mention relevant sponsors within these race reports alongside any other sponsor activity from the weekend.

Sponsor announcements

You should use your website to announce any partnership deal, but also to announce other important sponsor news. If you've chosen your sponsors correctly then you'll know that the people who visit your website will also be interested in the latest news from them.

These announcements might include product launches, events, trade shows and more. Again, when pitching website content to a sponsor, consider what your audience would like to hear about.

Dedicated sponsor pages

I mentioned before that it's good to offer sponsor branding on your website, but consider a dedicated page for a business willing to pay for it - or when you need to sweeten the deal.

How this looks is up to you but you could consider a Q&A with your sponsor, some background information, a few images and any video content you've created for it.

To get started, ask about the business, how it serves customers, what it loves about motorsport and so on. This makes it a bit more interesting than a basic sales page.

Downloadable content

Offer sponsors an easy way to download the latest promotional images of you and your car, photos from race weekends and any video footage you've been shooting.

A secret page on your website with a link to a Dropbox folder containing your newest images and information is all you need. This means you only have to update one place with your content and all your sponsors will be able to see it.

This makes it as easy as possible for them to download and share your content.

Lead magnets

A lead magnet is a downloadable product that's offered for free in order to obtain leads (you may have seen some of these on the

Racing Mentor website). For example, a fitness sponsor might offer a weight-lifting program for free in order to get people to sign up for its mailing list.

You could offer to either host this on your website or, at the very least, post about it on your blog.

If you host it, make sure it's exclusive to you as this will make your audience feel extra special. Think of it as giving your audience a gift, so it has to be something they'll actually want. The more desirable the download, the better.

This is a really good option if you know the sponsor is actively trying to build its email list. This tends to mean it has a good sales funnel in place to turn subscribers into buyers. Look at the sponsor's website to see if it's actively encouraging people to sign up and, also, take a look at whether it's capturing leads at events.

Many companies will jump at the chance to get more people to sign up to their lists, so this is a very powerful thing to be able to offer.

In terms of the practicalities of this on your website, there are a number of tools that can help you create landing pages designed to convert. Take a look at Racingmentor.com/resources for all the links.

Consider SEO

This is easier said than done when you know nothing about the subject. Make an effort to learn the basics and how to measure your site in terms of Domain Authority, Trust Flow and so on, as I mentioned earlier. Once you know how valuable your site is, this is something you can offer to sponsors that take their own SEO efforts seriously.

In short, Google measures links from authority websites. If you are classed as an authority and you link back to a sponsor's site, it's going to look good for its business.

17.

Press

If you're looking in the local newspaper for potential sponsors, you know these people are keen to reach a local audience. Offering press coverage locally, nationally, online and in a wide range of different press is so important to you as a racing driver - but you need to prove yourself first.

Get some press coverage that you can show off to potential sponsors. In the first instance, it only needs to be a couple of pieces of local coverage and perhaps one national piece, too, but you need to be confident you can deliver for your sponsors. The key here is to build relationships with journalists before you even start. Social media is a great tool for this.

Local Coverage

This is the most powerful tool in the arsenal of a club racing driver. You might be racing all over the country but you'll be picking up coverage in your local area. It's not just race reports you can get in the local press either - you can also work with your sponsor on events, announcements and local interest pieces. The scope for decent sponsor-focused coverage here is immense.

Again, think outside of the box and pitch a few ideas to a

potential sponsor that will not only hook it, but also show you know what you're talking about. It might be an initiative to get more young women interested in engineering using your race car, it might be inviting press along to a talk you're giving at an event for the sponsor's chosen charity or it might be a showcase of your locally-themed car livery.

Motorsport Press

If you do well, there's the chance you could get picked up by the motorsport press (and on television, if your series is televised). While this is very cool, there aren't always as many benefits to your sponsors unless they sell motorsport products or target fans of the sport.

You can work with the motorsport press on features beyond simple race reports. Think about what readers might want to know about the world of motorsport and work with your sponsors to make it happen.

Back in the earlier press section of this book, we talked about finding a hook and making yourself stand out from all the other racing drivers out there - this is still true when you're working on ways to promote your sponsors.

Lifestyle Press

This is something so few drivers pick up on and it's very desirable to businesses. While you might not be unique on a race weekend, you do have something special when it comes to stories for the fashion, fitness and lifestyle press. Start thinking about the coverage you could get in the glossy magazines you see in supermarkets.

When pitching as a journalist or for my clients, I'll go into a large supermarket and scoop up an armful of glossy mags to take back to my office. Just reading through them will often give me ideas. It can also be a great place to find potential new sponsors, because you know the people advertising in those mags would love some editorial coverage too.

Lifestyle magazines go way beyond what you find in your local supermarket or newsagent, too. There are so many online-only magazines, as well as those you might only find in niche stockists. Use Google to expand your knowledge of the press within your niche and get an idea of the kinds of stories they cover.

If you work with a PR, they'll probably already have the contacts needed but, failing that, look in the front of a magazine at the masthead and you'll find them there.

Online

Local, motorsport and lifestyle coverage online is just as important as print coverage. Especially if your sponsor is focused on its SEO efforts. Don't overlook this powerful tool - start sending your race reports, press releases and content ideas to online outlets too.

Trade Press

This can be your secret weapon when it comes to promoting your sponsors. You'll be hard-pressed to find a sector that doesn't have a trade or industry publication that's keen to accept news stories. In my experience, these publications are often quite easy to get into, and a news story in one of them reflects very well on your sponsors. Do your research before pitching to a business and find out what its relevant trade magazines are.

Trade magazines will often print good news stories, such as a tie-in between a racing driver and industry business, so this can be an easy win when it comes to coverage.

Build a press list of both print and online publications so you always have the email addresses to hand when you have something to send out.

18.

Events

This is most relevant to businesses that already attend and run events. Think about how they would benefit from the presence of a race car and driver. You should also think about what else you can do to help them maximise these events, be it in terms of coverage, attendence or lead capture.

That being said, there's no reason why you shouldn't pitch events to a business that hasn't tapped into this market just yet.

Trade Shows

A trade show is a wonderful chance for you to promote a business, draw people to your sponsor's stand and perhaps even offer a competition prize.

Find out which shows potential sponsors will be exhibiting at and offer to be there with your car to help drum up sales or assist with lead capture (for example, taking names and emails addresses for a competition). A trade show is also a good place to do Q&As, which you can promote online to draw people to the stand at a certain time.

You could even have a very special event where you uncover

a new car or livery. These timed events will help to draw large crowds at a specific time. Not only does this look great for your sponsor and will help it sell more, but it's also good for your profile.

> Giveaways are also an important part of trade shows, and a nice tactic for getting people to hand over their business card or email address. You could offer hot laps, merchandise or even on-track instruction to help your sponsor draw in the crowds.

Car Club Events

Whether you're part of a car club or are willing to join to promote a sponsor, this can be a great way to reach a wide range of people. Perhaps your race car fits nicely with a local club, or maybe your daily driver is perfect for one of the bigger national meet-ups.

There are so many ways you can work with a car club, from simply showing your car complete with sponsor logos to having a dedicated area where members can meet your sponsor and get special event discounts.

When planning something like this, consider the size of the event and how many people you'll potentially be able to reach. A lot of effort to reach a few hundred people might not be worth it, but similar effort to reach 5,000 could be.

Press Events

Anything you can do to introduce more people to your sponsor is good. Typically, press events need to have something special in order to draw in reporters from the big newspapers and magazines.

Think about what a journalist would get from an event. Usually, information isn't enough - you need to entice them with freebies or unusual experiences. A hot lap in your race car is a good start, but consider giving instruction to a small group in a track day car, or having a simulator in which journalists can compete to beat your fastest lap time.

Again, think outside the box and use your strengths - combined with activities that are relevant to your sponsor - to come up with interesting events that journalists and influencers will want to attend.

The end-goal of any press event should be for the press to write about their experiences while giving you and your sponsor a nice plug. Following up with press is important here, so don't just forget about them once the event is done and dusted - check in via email a week or two later to see when they might be running a story.

You could also invite bloggers and influencers along to these events; just make sure they have enough reach to warrant the cost.

Track Days

A track day has so many uses. It could be a way for sponsors to reward their customers or employees, it could serve as a competition prize that aids in lead capture or it could simply be a perk for a petrol-head business owner.

If you have the ability to put on track days - either instructing or giving hot laps - this should absolutely be used to help promote your sponsor.

Public Speaking

Not only is public speaking a great way to get yourself in front of new people, it can also be a great opportunity for your sponsors. Offer sponsors a few days of your time that can be used to speak at their events. The costs should be covered in their sponsorship package or included as an add-on.

You can help your sponsor to reach new people, engage with its customers and boost its brand. This is a fantastic chance for you to represent your partners in front of an audience.

If you've successfully built your profile as a racing driver, your words will also carry more weight than if they were to come from the CEO of a business. Not only that, but you'll be able to draw your own crowd to an event or talk.

Workshops

A workshop is a hands-on event that lets you get up close and personal with your community, sponsor stakeholders and motorsport fans. You might take guests through the basics of car maintenance, a race car wheel change or a sim racing session.

This is another great way to generate PR coverage, build an audience and reach new people.

Seasonal Events

Look for opportunities around seasonal events. For many sponsors this will be the usual Valentine's Day, Easter, Christmas and New Year events but you can start to think outside the box here, too.

If you work with a car company, consider something around new registrations. If you work with a fashion brand, get involved with its fashion week plans. There are plenty of ways your presence and race car could enhance an event, even if it's not directly motorsport-related.

Customer Engagement

It's so much easier and cheaper for a business to keep an existing customer happy than it is to find a new one. You can help to keep customers engaged by allowing them to follow your racing, get involved where possible and attend special events. Your sponsors want to better engage with their customers and you can give them those opportunities.

Employee Engagement

In many industries, retaining talent is a key part of running a successful business. For especially large businesses, employees can feel undervalued, so it's important for managers to give employees the kind of perks that keep them happily serving high-value clients.

Imagine working a really tough job with no rewards other than your monthly pay packet - that'd get soul destroying really quickly. Now, imagine that same tough job where you occasionally get to drive a race car, or get access to amazing motorsport hospitality. Way better, right?

Businesses want to hold onto their best staff because the recruitment process is lengthy and expensive. You can give businesses a myriad of wonderful ways to reward valuable employees.

Networking Events

Sometimes, you'll be in a good position to introduce your sponsors to other business owners who might be able to work with them. You might be able to introduce a sponsor to a supplier that saves money on something it needs, or you might be able to introduce the sales manager of a company you work with to a new high-value customer.

Dan Kirby, racing driver and owner of Trade Price Cars, has sponsored teams across motorsport, including in the British Touring Car Championship. When he raced in the BMW Compact Cup, paddock networking benefitted both his business and racing career. He says: "Being involved in motorsport has definitely paid off. When I started five years ago in the BMW Compact Cup, Trade Price Cars was on my car and I sold cars off the back of that branding.

"I also met a number of dealers through the BMW Compact Cup that I still buy cars off today. So, even though I don't race with them now, that relationship is still there and I buy two or three cars a month off them. When I quantify that value, it paid for my racing for those three years and I've got a great working relationship for as long as I'll be in business."

Networking will naturally happen in the paddock, but you should also consider setting up special events and networking dinners to help your sponsors get to know one another.

There's the chance to be especially savvy here as you could specifically target sponsors whose businesses will complement one another. This sets you up nicely to help them all make sales.

19.

Video Content

Video is a powerful tool in marketing a brand, be it yours or a partner's. Including a video on a landing page can increase conversions by 80%, and YouTube reports that mobile video consumption increases by 100% year-on-year. On top of that, 92% of viewers share videos with others, meaning it's one of the most efficient ways to reach new customers.

Whether a potential sponsor is new to video, dabbling in this kind of content or an expert, there's plenty you can offer. Premade videos that come with no extra cost to a sponsor are always appreciated, but you can also work with sponsors to create something big.

Vlogs

A vlog (also known as a video blog) is a great way to give people an insight into your life as a racing driver. It makes your audience feel like they're right there with you but also gives you a great platform to promote a sponsor.

This might be done really subtly, such as you drinking a sponsor's coffee in your morning routine, or it could be more obvious. You might introduce your viewers to the CEO of a business you work with, you might extol the benefits of a particular product or use a vlog to announce a new sponsor.

Once again, get creative, especially when you are pitching to a potential sponsor. You need to be able to show that you've thought about how your vlogs might impact a business and its goals.

Brand videos

Creating videos can be time-consuming, so if a brand is putting out regular content, you can offer something very special. You could offer to record videos that it can post on its channels - this is really valuable to a time-stretched business with budget to spend.

You could also offer to host brand videos. These are videos created either by your sponsor or by you in collaboration with the brand that you post on your website, YouTube channel or other social channels.

In these collaborative videos you might talk about a sponsor's products in a simple sales video, or you might go on an epic adventure to find out exactly how a foodie sponsor sources the ingredients for its natural protein bars, for example.

Having you present the video saves on hiring another presenter, and also increases the video's reach as you'll be tapping into your existing audience - all of whom could be potential customers, of course.

Instructional videos

If you have a particular skill, you could also share it in an instructional video. Perhaps your video shows people how to drift and includes details of your sponsor's range of sport tyres. Or, maybe you show people how to stretch before a long drive while wearing a sponsor's range of workout gear.

You could also create instructional videos for your sponsors to give their customers more insight in how to use a product. These could be cookery videos showing how to use a product as an ingredient, a demonstration of a new electronic device or a video showing how to install a car part.

The key to offering video content is to have something already in place that shows what you can do. I can't stress enough how important it is to work with a good videographer, as they can really elevate your work and show your dedication and professionalism to potential sponsors.

PART THREE

RESEARCHING SPONSORS

Consider this: you receive an email trying to sell you some car parts that don't fit your car. You're just going to ignore it, right? But an email talking about the increase in power from a part that is designed for your car and the way you drive - that's going to be a lot more interesting.

Unfortunately, pitching to sponsors isn't as simple as finding an email address and sending a message. You'll need to put a lot more work in than that but, thankfully, your success rate will also increase.

This is where most racing drivers are going wrong. It's important to research a business thoroughly before you pitch to it, because what works for one might not work for another. It's also important to show that you've thought about your pitch and tailored it to the business in mind.

From experience, I can confirm how annoying it is to receive a generic pitch. If someone is going to sell something to me, I want to know that they understand my business or are willing to ask the right questions to determine if they can help me.

Use your research - coupled with the ideas in the previous section - to come up with a bespoke plan for each business you pitch to.

20.

Determining Goals

A goal is something a business is actively working towards. For many, it's an increase in sales, for others it might be specific to a new product, and some might be aiming for increased brand awareness.

Understanding the goals of a business is important because, in your pitch, you need to tell a business owner exactly how you're going to help them achieve those goals.

How to identify a business's audience

You need to start by identifying a business's audience - also known as its target market. Who do they want to buy its products or services? Who is already buying its products or services?

Your first step should be to visit the company's website to get an idea of the look and feel of it. Take some time to brainstorm keywords and ideas that come to mind on seeing the website. Is it luxury, budget, mid-range? What are people visiting the site interested in? How old are they? Where do they live?

You can do similar research with specific products if the website is a little overwhelming .

Ask all these questions and write down some answers based on your initial research. Then, compare this information to the demographics of your audience. If the answers are the same then you're well-suited to working with this brand and could help it to reach new people.

If your answers are similar, then there's a good chance you can still work together. If your audiences are vastly different, you might need to look elsewhere.

How to identify its goals

Once you understand a business's audience, you need to work out what its goals might be. There are a number of ways you can do this, but you first need to get a sense of what it's doing to attract those customers.

Have a casual stalk of the company's social profiles, read a few blog posts and see where it has been mentioned online and in the media. You can do this with a simple Google search.

Where it's advertising, what it's writing about and how it's communicating with potential customers will tell you a lot about what the brand is trying to do.

For example, if your target business is advertising in a local glossy magazine, you know one goal it has is to reach people in your local area. If it's also talking enthusiastically about where it's based, then it's likely it also wants to be seen as a part of the community. If you've built a name for yourself in your local area, you're well-placed to help that business achieve its goals.

Similarly, if you see a potential sponsor exhibiting at a business to business (B2B) event, you know it's trying to sell its products or services to other businesses, while if the business has a presence at a consumer auto show, you know it's targeting regular buyers.

Brainstorm some goals

Take some time to write down some of a business's marketing activity, and brainstorm what kind of goals that activity is helping it to achieve. You're not going to be right every time but this exercise will give you a better sense of what a business is trying to do.

I've done this in this example table below for a fitness company.

Marketing activity	Potential goals
Fitness magazine advert	Sell more of the advertised product to fitness enthusiasts/athletes
Speaking at a CrossFit convention	Brand awareness establishing expertise in fitness/CrossFit/a talk topic
Social and blog posts about nutrition	Brand awareness establishing expertise in nutrition
Free downloadable guide to nutrition for weight lifters	Build an email list targeting weight lifters interested in nutrition; get new potential nutrition customers into the relevant sales funnel

How a business's goals fit your offering

Once you have a list of some potential goals, you need to consider what part you could play in helping the business reach them.

Let's stick with the fitness angle for now, but this could work similarly for motorsport, a local business, someone in fashion or a brand you're interested in from another industry.

Look at the goals you've written down and ask yourself these questions:

> » Do I have access to kind of people this business is trying to target?
>
> » Can I help make sales?
>
> » Can I help make people more aware of this brand?
>
> » Are there any unique ways in which I can help this business grow its email list/get more people to its event/insert other goal here?

Ideally, you need to answer 'yes' to all of these questions to have the best benefit to a business. Once you have your yes or no answer, ask yourself how.

Yes, you can help raise awareness of this brand, but how? List out the reasons, which could look something like this:

> » Because you have a large (be specific, add numbers), relevant audience on Twitter
>
> » Because you make fitness videos for YouTube that reach X subscribers
>
> » Because you've got an upcoming speaking gig about motorsport nutrition

These answers will give you the details of what you should offer a business. To work out how your offering can benefit a business, refer back to its goal.

For example, if the business is looking to increase sales of a specific fitness product and you already have people clicking affiliate links to fitness products on your blog, you know for sure you can sell it. You can do this by posting about the products on your blog and social media. The benefit of this activity to the business is that you will directly help it sell more. All you need to do to back this up is give the business stats on social followings, what sells well via blog posts, sales figures and monthly visitor stats.

If you answer 'no' to any of the first set of questions, you can ask yourself, *"why not?"* to get an idea of how you can improve your offering. This might be a quick fix, or you might need to work more on your audience and niche. If you've answered 'no' to a lot of the questions above, perhaps that particular business isn't right for you.

21.

Approaching Businesses you Know

This is, by far, the easiest way to land a sponsorship deal, but it relies heavily on how much networking you've been doing and how many business owners you actually have in your black book (or on social media).

These businesses are often called hot leads - they're people you've already had dealings with who know what you can do. Usually, all it takes is a well-placed email to convince them to sponsor you.

Even if you do have a few of these hot leads floating around, don't take them for granted. They'll be the easiest deals to land but will still take a little work.

You still need to do your research

Even if you've met with a business, talked goals and bonded over your love for motorsport, you still need to show them that a partnership with you makes real business sense.

Do your research - as you would with any other business - before writing your pitch. The only difference is that you have a slight head start in terms of what you know about the business, the owner and what they're trying to achieve.

An introduction is powerful

Even if you don't know a business owner personally, an introduction from a mutual contact is going to give you a lot more sway than if you go in cold. Building trust is difficult when you make first contact with an unsolicited email but, if you can slipstream in on someone else's trust, you're in a good position to make a sale.

So, if a contact is keen to support you but doesn't have the money to, ask if they'd be willing to make an introduction to other business owners.

Once you've been introduced - or before, if you can - do your research on this company and ask your contact what else they know. Use this to inform your pitch but don't spend too long over it, otherwise the business owner may forget who you are and who introduced you.

As you've been reading through this book you may have been mentally (or physically) making notes of potential people and businesses that might be a good fit - split these out into hot, warm and cold leads.

The hot leads are where you should focus your attention as you're much more likely to land that sale.

Don't just think of businesses you've used in the past and have a relationship with, but consider what opportunities could come from family and close friends. Even if you don't know any business owners, if the people you're close to can make introductions, you've got powerful warm leads ready and waiting.

Hot and warm leads are worth a lot more of your time than a cold approach, as your success rate will be higher. Again, this is why building a rapport with business owners is important before you pitch.

22.

How to Find
Potential Sponsors

Eventually, you'll want to look beyond your hot and warm leads to start finding new businesses to target. These are typically known as cold leads as it's unlikely you'll have an existing relationship with them.

The best advice I can give here is to be shit-hot with your research. I know it can be tempting to blanket email everyone you find in the Autosport International Show directory, but that's a waste of time because everyone is doing it. You need to stand out.

When you're doing your research, get involved with this business on social media. Reply to a post on its Facebook page, comment on its Instagram story, post something informative/ witty/helpful under the CEO's latest LinkedIn post or send a tweet saying how much you loved a recent article about the business.

This activity might not go the whole way to creating the kind of rapport you need to classify the business as a warm lead, but there's a chance your name will be recognised when your email pops up in the right inbox.

This whole chapter gives advice on finding potential sponsors in places that give you a sense of what their goals might be, so the research and pitch process is much easier.

Using Magazines and Newspapers

A great way to find potential sponsors is to go through magazines and look at the adverts that have been placed there. Not only do you know that those businesses have budget, but you can also get a good sense of their goals based on the type of magazine and its demographic.

You can work out the audience of a magazine or newspaper by following the methods outlined in the section on your audience.

Looking at adverts

First, you need to pick up a selection of magazines that your target audience would read (these will be the same as the magazines you pick up to research your own press opportunities). Remember, you don't just have to stick to motorsport magazines.

Start by looking through the adverts and getting a sense of the types of businesses advertising there. If a particular advert jumps out at you for its design or content, then it's a good place to start.

Follow the advice earlier in this book about determining a business's goals, and make sure to include the reasons why it's advertising in this particular magazine.

For example, a business advertising in *Fast Car* magazine is usually targeting petrol-heads who love modded cars and enjoy working on their own. If you have a similar audience who are following your race car build, you can help that business reach more people to raise brand awareness and increase product sales.

> If you want to watch me talk you through advert research, visit Racingmentor.com/adresearch.

The best thing about these businesses is that you can determine exactly what kind of budget they have. The rate cards for most magazines and newspapers are readily available online and, if they're not, all it usually takes is a call to the relevant advertising department. Although, perhaps don't tell them you're trying to poach their clients...

Looking at articles

The articles in a magazine or newspaper can also help. Look at the brands that are mentioned or what businesses the featured experts are from - these could also be good prospects, as the target audience is likely the same as those taking out adverts in the magazine. While these editorial mentions aren't usually paid for, unless it's an advertorial, you can still get a sense of what a business is trying to achieve with its press coverage.

An article can also make a good opener for a soft pitch. When you email a business, you can tell it that you saw/enjoyed/were moved by its article in the magazine.

An opener like this shows you've done your research and are familiar with the brand. It also shows that you're a human being who isn't sending emails en masse.

How to Find Potential Sponsors at Events

Attending events is an important part of picking up sponsorship. At the very least you should be attending networking events in your local area, but you should also look further afield to trade shows, national networking events and conferences.

Of course, the type of events you attend depends on your target audience and the kind of sponsor you're trying to attract. For example, there's no point attending a classic car show when you race a modern GT car. While you might be able to find one or two relevant potential customers, you'd be better off using your time and energy in a place where you'll find a lot more of them.

How to get contact details

Your goal at any event should be to get contact details and make yourself known to decision-makers. If the opportunity arises to pitch for sponsorship, go for it, but don't force it. Your goal here is to make contact and build a rapport rather than make a sale on the day. The business owners at these events - especially trade shows - are being pitched to left, right and centre, so you're more likely to stand out if you gather some contact details and wait.

If you show a genuine interest in the business and can build a rapport with the decision-maker (usually the owner or marketing manager) you're going to stand out from the crowd, as most drivers would barrel in with a generic pitch.

The key here is to ask questions and show genuine interest. If you need to, research some of the exhibitors or guests ahead of time and prepare some questions.

Ask about their products, what they do, how they started, how business is or why they chose to develop a product in a certain way. Share what you do and relate it to their answers. Then, ask if you can take their card while handing over yours.

Wait to pitch

In waiting to pitch, you give yourself time to do adequate research on the company. You also allow yourself to build a rapport with the decision-maker without scaring them off with an instant face-to-face pitch.

If they remember you for good reasons ("that driver was really interested in how we made our product") rather than bad ones ("why are racing drivers always begging for money?"), you're better placed to write a convincing pitch that actually gets looked at.

Further research

Once you're back from the event and have the cards of a few good potential customers, make some notes on your conversations and any important points that could help you develop a winning sponsorship pitch. Then, go on to research the business and its goals as outlined earlier in this section.

Networking events

Networking events are a little different to trade shows and conferences. People are there to meet business contacts, sell and be sold to so you've got a little more wiggle room when it comes to pitching.

My advice, though, would be to go easy on the pitch. Don't be afraid to let people know what you're doing, what you're racing and that you're looking for partners - but don't outright ask anyone to agree to a sponsorship deal there and then.

Instead, show interest and ask questions. Find out what you can about a business and what it offers. You'll probably be asked a lot of questions, too, so make sure you have a deep understanding of your audience and what you can offer to a business.

It may also be worth reassuring people that you're offering more than a sticker on a car, as you're likely to meet people who have sponsored motorsport before and got nothing back from it.

How to Find Potential Sponsors Online

While personally meeting someone is the best way to build a rapport, it's absolutely possible to find sponsors online - you just need to right approach.

Via social media

In building your online empire, you will no doubt have come across businesses that could make great partners for your racing. If you have businesses following you, it's likely they'll already know a bit about who you are and what you do. There's a reason they've followed you.

In a lot of cases it's not obvious exactly why they've followed you, but you can still use it as an opener in any pitch email. Thank them for following you on social media and say how much you've enjoyed their posts (I assume you're following back at this point).

Looking at what a business is posting on social media can help you to craft an opening question that shows your interest in the business. Some ideas are:

- » I saw you had a new product launch last week, how did it go?
- » I really enjoyed your tweets from the London Motor Show, how was it?
- » How did your event go last weekend? It looked great!

Again, proper research is important here to maximise the opportunities for the business, but it should be easier to open a dialogue than if you went in cold.

> I like to contact potentials via direct message, especially on LinkedIn or Twitter. I open with something about their content, such as what I've enjoyed or something I'd like to know more about.

I might not directly ask for the best person to send a pitch to right away but, eventually, after building a rapport, I'll mention that I have a pretty cool opportunity and would love to run it by someone. That's when I ask for an email address and people are usually willing to hand one over.

This is a much better approach than searching for one online as you'll usually get the direct email of the decision-maker.

Searching online

If you've exhausted your list of businesses you know, have been introduced to and who follow you on social media, it's time to start searching for new prospects.

Bear in mind that a cold approach is far less likely to prove successful, but it is possible. I've had a lot of great opportunities come my way from cold pitching businesses (including something worth £21,000), so don't discount it.

> They key here is to take your time and, where possible, still try to create that rapport.

A good place to start is with local businesses; a Google search will bring up plenty of businesses in your surrounding area. The good thing about going local is that you instantly have something in common with that business, and it's (hopefully) going to be more willing to support a local athlete.

You should also search for businesses that fall within your secondary niche or share the same audience as you. As these businesses pop up, do some initial research: what does its website look like and who does it target? Does it have social media channels? Does it use video? If it looks like it could be a good prospect, add this business to your list for further research.

Finding contact details

While it might be easy to find some contact details on a website, they're probably not the ones you need. In order to get your pitch noticed, you need to contact the decision-maker. This might be the business owner or a marketing manager, but it's unlikely you'll find their email address on the website.

You need to make a phone call. A lot of racing drivers are reluctant to do this, and I get it. I had to get over phone anxiety when I was working as a PR but, when making sponsorship sales calls, I've never had someone be rude to me. Once you do a couple of these calls you'll be well into the swing of things.

I'd recommend batching these calls, especially if you're a little nervous. Get 10 done in half an hour or so and each one will seem easier than the last.

Sometimes, speaking to the right person can be like pulling teeth, but the key is to be nice to the gatekeepers (receptionists, secretaries, switchboard operators and assistants).

Start simple and explain you have an opportunity that could reach [target market] and ask who might be the best person to email the details to. You might get palmed off with a generic email address, but try to get the address of someone real so you have a name you can ask for when you next call.

Researching goals

Once you've found a business and have some contact details, you need to do your research. Just in the same way you would with a business you know well, take some time to look at marketing activity and work out how you could contribute to its goals.

If you're not sure how to structure your research for hot, warm and cold leads, there's a sample research sheet available at Racingmentor.com/research.

PART FOUR

THE PITCH

A pitch can be split into a number of parts, from the initial research through to the follow-ups. This section will cover exactly what you need to do to impress a business, show it how you can work for it and seal the deal. The key elements to any pitch are as follows:

- » **Research** - Covered earlier in this book
- » **The hook** - Something that piques the reader's interest
- » **The offer** - They key benefits to working with you
- » **The info** - Who you are, what you race in, why they should support you
- » **The numbers** - A quick run-down of the important numbers and stats in terms of reach, audience and coverage
- » **The call-to-action** - What you want the business to do next
- » **The follow ups** - A series of follow-ups to ensure you get a firm yes or no from your prospect

When I started out finding sponsorship for karters - and then my own racing team - I made mistakes, but I've honed my approach and have seen my success rate triple. The information covered so far in this book comes from many years of experience as a businessperson, salesperson, sponsor, team boss, journalist and motorsport coach.

Before you launch into your pitch, make sure you have all the relevant information - not just about the business you're targeting, but also about you and your audience.

With each pitch you write, it'll get easier and easier to understand a business and how you can bring real-world benefit to its bottom line. Your first pitch might take you a long time and you'll probably want to get feedback from friends, family and friendly business owners, but it does get easier and you will get quicker.

This method might seem time-consuming but it's worth it in the long-run.

23.

What Businesses Want

Understanding what businesses want is a large part of writing a pitch. Obviously, you're not a mind-reader (if only!) but if you can get a sense of what businesses generally respond to in a pitch, you're off to a good start.

Consider who you're talking to

If you can find a business owner who is a motorsport fan, then you're going to have much more success selling the benefits of marketing their business with race cars - but don't rely on this as your only hook. You still need to offer something valuable to a business.

Dan Kirby, owner of Trade Price Cars, explains why getting involved with the British Touring Car Championship made sense: "Obviously being a motorsport fan, that was the initial interest. But often I'm looking, as with any advertising, for ways we can boost our brand in something we love doing.

"For us, motorsport and selling cars worked hand in hand. Everyone needs a car, but we wanted to tap into the audience of petrolheads in the motorsport community - both competitors and the wider audience of fans."

Make it easy

I spoke to Vikki Little, an automotive marketing expert with more than 20 years' experience in the industry. Over the years she's helped with sponsorship activation for a wide range of brands. She has this advice for racing drivers looking to impress with a pitch: "Businesses may be nervous about the time and money they think is required to make the most of the sponsorship, and they might not have the resources and/or time to meet this."

The thought of sponsoring a racing driver might be daunting and seem like a lot of work to a small business, even if it has the budget in place to make it happen. If it seems like that might be the case, it's your job to assure the business owner that you're going to do all of the legwork.

Perhaps you'll pop to their offices to pick up leaflets to distribute at the track, or maybe you'll write up the blog post for their website about the partnership. Think how you can make a business owner's life easier while helping them to bring in sales.

Become more than just an ROI calculation

While return on investment will be important for a sponsor, you need to look beyond that. You need to become part of its team, living and breathing the products you're promoting as if they were your own. Peter Szarafinski, head of media relations at LIQUI MOLY understands this all too well. He says: "People do not suffer from too little choice when buying products. To make sure that it is our products people decide on, and not the ones from our competitors, we have to stand out.

"Basically, you can stand out by price or by brand. A brand is something which you do not create by yourself but it is something which is born in the people's minds. This implies that people need to know our brand; this is why brand awareness is so important for us."

> Understanding a brand and how to communicate its story is a very important part of being a brand ambassador.

Don't be afraid to brag

Businesses want to know they're backing a winner, so you need to be confident in your results both on track and as an ambassador.

Ryan from Car Keys says: "Maybe this sounds a bit harsh, but most businesses would be more willing to sponsor a driver who is consistently finishing on the podium than somebody who wallows around the bottom of the results table.

"At least you can spot that there's potential there to move up into bigger racing series, so you might be more inclined to sponsor an unknown driver if you know that they get good results."

If you're winning, shout about it. If you're not, find the positives in your career and shout about those. You should also be confident in saying how much benefit you've brought to other sponsors.

How to Find Out What Businesses Want

For the most part, you'll need to work on instinct, but you can get an idea of what will impress a business from your research. As you send more pitches and get more feedback (positive and negative), you'll be able to better hone your approach to suit your career so far and what you're offering.

A note on the language you use

Even though you're drafting a business pitch, you don't necessarily have to use formal language. Try and match the tone of the business you're sending the email to.

While you might want to keep it formal for a high-end, corporate bank, you can probably allow a little more personality to come through when pitching to a young startup targeting teenagers.

No matter the tone of your pitch, make sure you come across as a real human - this is what you want businesses to buy into.

24.

Using Your Research to Form a Pitch

Here's what you need to know ahead of writing your pitch:

- » Business goals
- » Name and position of decision-maker
- » Previous sponsorship activity
- » Other marketing activity
- » Target audience
- » Product offering
- » Previous and upcoming events

Knowing all of this can help you to determine what's important to the business and how you can help it reach its goals.

Write down these points above and list out what you know about a potential sponsor within each category. If you have any gaps, try to fill them in. It might be that you can't find out this information, even with expert research skills - in which case, don't spend too much time hunting online for the answers. Research is important but don't use it as an excuse to procrastinate. Believe me, that's a fine line to tread.

If you can't find out what you need online, you've got a good opening question either on social media or in an email.

How your offering can benefit them

If you're targeting a business that's very active in the events scene, regularly attending conferences and trade shows, then you need to think about how what you offer can benefit this activity.

The obvious answer for this example is a race car to draw crowds to a trade stand, increase engagement and build email lists. Also consider an offering of hot laps in your race car to encourage people to sign up to a mailing list, take part in a competition or drop their business card off on the stand.

How to jot all this down for each sponsor

The table on page 123 looks at sponsor activities, what you can offer and the benefits to the business. Try and recreate something similar ahead of creating your pitch.

Packages

By creating a table like the one opposite, you'll start to get an idea of what kind of package you can build for each sponsor. This should also hammer home the point that a generic package which only lists features is pretty much worthless, and won't get picked up.

When considering the costs for a package, there's two ways to think about it. Firstly, how much money do you need for your sponsorship? It's perfectly acceptable to start at this point and consider if you're offering enough within your package to give value to that business for that kind of money.

The second method is to consider how much time all this activity would take you. You might want to charge per day for your time, per social post or per hour. Most of the high profile drivers I know charge a day rate - this can vary from £500 into the thousands, and it really is up to you and the confidence you have in your abilities as an influencer.

Business activity	What you offer	Benefits to the business
Competitions on social media	Hot laps and race-day hospitality	A chance to offer unique money-can't-buy experiences to competition winners to further grow social followings and increase brand awareness
Videos showing the sponsor's products in action	High-quality videos shared to an audience of car enthusiasts.	A chance to reach a highly-engaged audience of X with minimal effort using existing video content
Advertising in a local glossy magazine	Coverage in the local press	Save money on advertising with editorial mentions in local magazines and newspapers
Events for sponsor's customers	Talks and access to the race car	Engage customers with a race car at events, which they can photograph and post on social media with a custom hashtag (further increasing reach). Draw in more customers with interesting talks about what it's like to drive a powerful race car

You need to understand what you're worth and the value you can bring. Doing sponsorship properly is a lot of work for you as a racing driver, and £100 per day probably isn't a good reflection of what you're doing and the value you're bringing.

The best approach is to combine the two. Maybe you need £10,000 to cover travel, entry fees and tyres for the season. You know that the activity you're proposing is going to cost about 10 days of your time across the year, as well as a few longer events where you'll need to transport your car across the country.

While your time is valuable, you don't necessarily have to take your day rate out of your sponsorship money, but you should account for travel costs as well as the cost for transporting your car. Sometimes you can absorb these costs from a large sponsorship fee. For example, if someone is willing to give you £100,000 for your season, there's no point in charging £101,000 to cover some travel.

The next thing you need to consider is value. Even if the actual work you're going to be doing doesn't come to £10,000 (or whatever you're asking for), consider the results the business will be getting.

Swapping advertising for editorial coverage could be worth thousands alone if you're targeting a large glossy magazine.

The amount of people you could help draw into a trade stand could bring in a number of new sales and, if the average sale for that business is quite high, that could easily cover a large chunk of your sponsorship money.

Learning the value of an average sale for a potential sponsor can put you in a good place when it comes to negotiating. Don't be afraid to ask this question.

When building a package, think about the business's goals,

your time and the end result. Don't be afraid to ask for what you're worth; you can always haggle later.

Another sales strategy is to price high. If you go to a very interested small business asking for £30,000 after selling all the benefits and they can't afford it, they're likely to jump at the chance to work with you for £10,000.

A note on value

Perceived value is an important thing - there are a lot of businesses that will be more willing to pay £10,000 for a package than they would £1,000. The simple reason is because we don't trust cheap things. How can businesses be sure that they're going to get any results if it seems cheap?

This is a great reason to charge a larger amount for an all-singing-all-dancing package tailored to that specific sponsor. Don't undervalue what you can offer and make sure the business can see the value you can bring.

When I was running Turn Eight Racing, we were just another Porsche Championship team, but we did our best to come across as so much more than that. We had matching teamwear, appeared regularly in the local and national press, had a wrapped 924 and a whole slew of sponsor stickers. We managed to raise our perceived value (and real value) so we could get sponsorship.

25.

The Importance of Making Each Pitch Personal

Goals, audience and activity will be different for each business, even if they're in similar industries. You wouldn't pitch a product to Tesco in the same way you would to Waitrose.

The same goes for any business you're targeting. Not only that, but no business owner wants a generic, impersonal pitch - they're annoying and will get chucked in the bin (or digitally dragged to it). If you can show that you've really thought about a business and how you can work closely together, most business owners will be impressed and will give you more time of day for your efforts.

A lot of this is covered in the previous chapter and how you build a package, but it's more than just that.

Here are some tips for adding that personal touch into your pitch:

- » Address the decision-maker by name
- » Reference their products/services/advertising campaigns/ events
- » Reference their target market and any insights you have about them

» Mention any previous experience you have with the brand - perhaps you're a long-term customer

» Reference important dates, for example: "I know you're planning on attending on the Professional Motorsport World event, perhaps I can pop by the stand for a chat."

This should all come from your research. If you're struggling with ways to make your pitch more personal and targeted, you probably need to familiarise yourself with the brand.

If your research hasn't been enough to help you get to know the brand and the decision-maker, you need to dive deeper or move on. Get yourself to one of the business's events, buy its flagship product or call the CEO for a chat (easier said than done, I'm aware).

26.

Sales Tips for Racing Drivers

If you don't have a sales background this can be really tricky and, if you're not used to getting on the phone and pestering people, it's going to be even harder to get in touch with those that truly could benefit from what you're doing.

If you want to be successful as a racing driver, you need money, and to get money you either a) have to be rich already, or b) need to learn how to sell. Here are some tips to help you achieve success:

Stay positive and believe in yourself

If you think about how much you hate sales, you'll go into every call/meeting feeling like you can't win. Commit to a positive attitude at all times, not just when speaking to sponsors but throughout your career. You also need to believe in yourself - if you go into a meeting thinking that you're going to fail, the prospective sponsor will be able to pick up on it.

Set goals and achieve them

Split your goals up into two camps: the thing you want (long-term goal), and how you're going to get it (short-term goals).

These might be sales goals, the goal to make 10 phone calls in a day or a goal for secured sponsorship deals by the end of the month. Be realistic but don't give up until you get there.

Rebecca Jackson is always my benchmark for goal setting. No matter what she's going for, she makes a plan and she achieves it. Whether she's set out to race at a prestigious track such Le Mans or Monaco, to achieve a certain championship position or smash a business goal, she gets things done.

She says: "When I set big goals, I see them as something I'm going to do, no questions asked - that way I'm certain within myself they will happen.

"Once you have a big goal, break it down into what you're going to do to get there, either in stages or shorter-term goals. You need a timeline, too, so you know when your big goal or mini goals will happen.

"The only person who can hold the reins in your life to get you to where you need to go is you. You guide the reins to the right places and find the right people to assist you with your quest, but it falls on you to make it all happen. Team this with belief in yourself alongside confidence, analysis and a strong work ethic, and you'll got exactly where you want to go and do exactly what you set out to achieve."

Understand the customer

Your sponsors are your customers so, when going into a sale, you need to already know the customer inside out and, anything you don't know, you need to learn from them. By asking the right questions, you can uncover their true needs.

When a potential sponsors says: "We need to get more people to buy from us at events," they might not mean that. What they might mean is: "People don't know who we are so they don't find us at events." When building a rapport with a decision-maker, make sure you ask the right questions to really understand their pain points and how you can help.

Sell to help

Yes, sponsorship will help all your dreams come true but, if you think about anything other than how you can help the customer in a pitch, you're going to fail. Occasionally you'll find a sponsor that just wants to support you, but this still helps that business. It will get tax relief on that money, is often fulfilling corporate social responsibility requirements and the company will feel good for supporting someone it believes in.

Establish relationships

Treat your sponsors as you'd want to be treated. If you can establish a rapport with someone they're more likely to continue any partnership beyond the initial agreement.

You should also establish relationships with people who might not be able to sponsor you now, but would be interested in the future. Don't just drop someone if they can't front the cash - stay in touch.

Be prepared

Before every meeting or sales call, be prepared with imagery, facts and figures, questions, openers and answers. You should also have an idea of what objections the potential sponsor might have because it's important to tackle these as they come up.

Follow up, follow up, follow up

This is where most drivers fall down. Don't just send an email or make one call - you need to follow-up. Emails get missed and voicemails forgotten about. Be persistent.

Be memorable

There are some businesses out there that have racing drivers coming to them all the time with pitches for sponsorship. You need to stand out and you need to be memorable. You might do this through humour, with a unique look or simply by being the most valuable and professional. Look to others to see what works but don't do the same thing, because you'll never get noticed.

27.

The Pitch Format

How you format your pitch will likely vary with each potential sponsor you contact, the reason being because sometimes you'll have been passed the contact details from a mutual contact and other times you'll be going in cold. Sometimes you'll be contacting a very playful business, which warrants a more relaxed tone-of-voice; sometimes you'll be contacting a big corporate that requires slightly more formal language.

Tailor your pitch to each business and you'll see your reply rate go through the roof.

Start with the hook

The hook is something that draws the decision-maker in and makes them think "wow, that's interesting." It might be a fact about you and your racing but, more likely, it's about what you can offer the business.

The hook completely depends on the business and its goals.

Some examples are:

» Do you want to reach 20,000 people this week for less than the cost of an advert in our local newspaper?

- » I have an opportunity that will help you to improve customer engagement with race cars.
- » We share the same audience and I'm willing to give you access to mine.
- » I noticed that you're targeting people in [area/niche] and I'd like to help you reach more of them.

How out-there you are with your hook depends on the business you're contacting. You can be a little more over-the-top with a business known for its innovative marketing activity than you could be with a bank, for example.

Tell them exactly what you're offering

Sometimes it's not appropriate to go in with your full package (true of a number things in life, I suppose...). While it can be tempting to craft a genius package for a business, you might scare it off before you've really had the chance to sell it on your offering.

In a cold email, I'd be inclined to list the benefits and few specific marketing activities to pique the potential customer's interest, but tell them you'd love to present the full package to them in person or on a call.

There are times where you can jump in with exactly what you're offering and the benefits to the business along with a cost; I've landed sponsorship deals this way with business owners that I've already built a rapport with at events. There's already a trust there, so they're more receptive to a bold approach complete with figures and costs.

Use your common sense and judge the situation. Do you have enough of a rapport with a business that you think they'll be an easy sell, or do you think it'll take a bit more wining and dining?

Include your personal details in the middle

Most racing drivers will start with who they are, and it causes a lot of businesses to just blandly skim-read the whole thing. Seeing that you're a racing driver who 'needs support' just sounds like someone who is begging for money.

Of course it's important that you're a champion with multiple impressive results, but there are so many other racers out there with similar credentials. Your press coverage and audience should speak for how awesome you are.

Talk about who you are, what you race, where it takes place and if it's on TV. Keep this section brief - when you meet a potential sponsor or get a contact on the phone, that's the time to say more about yourself.

End with the call-to-action

What do you want a business to do next? A phone call or meeting is usually the most obvious option but you have the chance to invite them to races, take them for dinner or get coffee.

End with something like this:

- » What does your schedule look like for a chat next week? I'm free Monday-Wednesday.
- » I'll be in your area next week, could I pop in on Monday or Wednesday?
- » I'd love to tell you more about this, can I give you a call tomorrow?
- » I have a race coming up next weekend - I'd love to show you exactly what I could do for your business. Let me know if you'd like to come along.

Over the page, you'll find a sample cold email template that will help you to hook a potential sponsor.

Sample cold email template

Dear [NAME OF DECISION-MAKER],

I've been looking at your recent [ACTIVITY/ADVERT/EVENT] and noticed we share the same audience. I'd love to give you access to mine to help you further increase those local sales.

I have a highly-engaged audience of car enthusiasts in [AREA]. My content reaches 20,000 people per month. As a racing driver, I have access to a number of interesting marketing tools that could help you increase online conversations, boost customer engagement and ultimately make more sales of [PRODUCT].

I'm currently racing in [CHAMPIONSHIP] and have built a loyal audience around my [TYPE OF RACE CAR]. I'm just coming from my fifth win of the season and have picked up press coverage worth £30,000 for my partners over the last six months.

I've got some great ideas for ways in which we could work together that I'd love to discuss with you. When would you be free for a call next week?

Kind regards,

[YOUR NAME]
[YOUR CONTACT DETAILS AND WEB ADDRESS]

28.

Nailing your Call-to-Action

Because the call-to-action is so important, it's worthy of its own chapter.

Get this right and you will have the business emailing back with a time and date for a call. The trick is to make it as easy as possible for someone to talk to you.

Popping into a sponsor's office or arranging a phone/video call are the easiest ways to speak to someone. Depending on the business, you may need to tailor your approach. Someone that keeps a tight schedule may need you to be flexible when it comes to a time to chat.

Consider what next step is best for the business you're contacting and then use that as a call-to-action.

For example, if you've spoke to a business owner at an event who confessed their love for iced coffee, offer to buy them one in your call-to-action.

This is why knowing something about the business you're contacting is so important. I once offered to make car-shaped biscuits for a company in the hope that it'd entice them into meeting with me. Suffice to say, it worked, and they even told me it was my biscuit offer that drew them in.

Because of this, I now often bring cakes or biscuits to events and meetings. In Racing Mentor colours, of course.

29.

Do you Need a Sponsorship Proposal?

In my experience, the answer to this question is 'not always'. I've landed deals from a simple email with a few bullet points.

However, standing out from the crowd is important so, if you can design something visually striking and update it for each sponsor you speak to, you're probably onto a winner.

Let your email do the talking

Your emails should hook the decision-maker and sell them into the idea of working with you. Your sponsorship proposal document (also known as a pitch deck or pitch document) should be there to outline the specific packages available, and give more information on who you are and what you race.

Don't send any attachments in the first instance

While it can be tempting to send a fancy document in the first instance, my advice would be to hold fire. Any attachment, especially from an email address outside of the decision-maker's contacts list, can be flagged as spam by corporate email systems.

You're best to simply send an introductory email. Feel free to link to your proposal (using Dropbox or SlideShare) or simply offer to send it over if they're interested.

Don't rely on it

Don't assume that sending a pretty proposal will win over any potential sponsors. Most of the time, a personal email that shows how much you know about the business can be far more impressive.

A proposal should act as a backup for when a business wants to know more but isn't quite ready to meet.

Present it in person

One thing that's far, far, far better than emailing a proposal document is to present it in person. Make sure your document is available as slides so you can show it off to someone when the opportunity arises.

Not only is it easier to hook someone face-to-face, you also have the opportunity to answer any questions they might have or tackle any objections. Even the best-prepared pitch in the world can't account for some of the weird questions businesses might ask.

Always push for a meeting where you can go into more detail if someone is interested.

What to Include in a Proposal Document

At the start of this section we looked at what the pitch process should include. Your proposal document should be a beautiful representation of all these elements. Here's what to include:

» **The hook** - Why are you different and how are you going to do more than another racing driver or influencer?

» **The offer** - They key benefits to working with you, specific to that business

» **The info** - Who you are, what you race in, why they should support you

» **The numbers** - A quick run-down of the important numbers and stats in terms of reach, audience and coverage
» **The packages** - Some information on the packages available and the general benefits of each element

A note on design

I am generally quite put off by ugly proposal documents (let's face it, I'm shallow). I can't say that all business owners will feel the same, but you put yourself in a much better position if you can create something that looks professional and attractive.

I'd always recommend hiring a designer, but I know that's not always practical for the cash-strapped racing driver. The easiest way to do this yourself is using presentation software. Think Powerpoint or Keynote for Windows and Mac users respectively, but there are also decent free versions available from Libreoffice and OpenOffice.

Create something simple and don't go over-the-top on crazy fonts or image placements - all you need to do is export as a PDF to be able to attach it to an email. You're also a step ahead if a business wants a proper presentation of what you can offer.

30.

The Email Follow-up

The point where racing drivers fall down is the follow-up. Have you ever received a message from a friend and forgotten to reply, only to then remember that you forgot when they next message you? We've all been there, and sending sponsorship emails is exactly the same.

Even I'm guilty of this; I get so many emails a day that it's often hard to stay on top of them. I deeply appreciate people who follow-up to remind me that I had every intention to reply before I got distracted by rewatching old Formula One races.

A follow-up message reminds an interested business that you sent an intriguing email, it nudges less interested businesses to give you some sort of reply and helps those sitting on the fence to make a decision. In some cases, your first email may have never been received, so in following-up you're ensuring that hasn't happened.

Link it to something relevant

While it's fine to just email to see if the person got your email, it's better if you can link it to something. Again, it's important to show interest in the business. You might mention a piece you saw about the business on BBC Breakfast, or an interesting article you read about its industry.

Take an interest and show your knowledge; it's also a good chance to add a "by the way, did you have a chance to look at my previous email?" There is a knack to getting this right and, if your email sounds insincere, just keep it simple.

Update the potential

If it feels right, take some time to update your contact on your racing, or any events you're attending. You might tell them about a slew of trophies you picked up, or how you're looking forward to speaking at a conference for another sponsor.

Giving this extra information serves to offer a small, natural piece of information about you. It shows that you're a real person with ambition, expertise and personality.

A simple follow-up

I've just seen that you've [WON AN AWARD/LAUNCHED A NEW PRODUCT/APPEARED ON TV] and wanted to say congratulations!

I also wondered if you'd had a chance to talk a look at the email I sent over last week regarding some ideas for ways in which I could introduce you to my audience. I know they'd be interested in what you have to offer.

Let me know if you're free for a call this week to discuss.

Congratulations once again. Have a great day!

31.

The Phone Call Follow-up

This is a really important part of the pitch process. Again, emails get missed and forgotten about so it makes perfect sense to call and check up on the status of the email. It's also a good chance to build that rapport with the decision-maker, something that's very important if you've sent a cold pitch.

Getting past the gatekeeper

Often you'll have to get past a receptionist, secretary or assistant before you can speak to the decision-maker. It's often the job of these employees to decide which calls are important enough to get through.

Firstly, be nice to the gatekeeper as they hold your fate in their hands; explain the opportunity and ask to speak to the decision-maker. It's likely that they'll be busy or won't want to be disturbed, so ask the gatekeeper for their help setting up a phone meeting.

The key here is ask for their help - everyone wants to feel important and helpful so it's likely that you'll get the help you need if you're polite and professional. At the very least, see if you can schedule an appointment that suits the decision-maker and the person you're speaking to.

If you get the right vibe, you could even ask the gatekeeper to look through your pitch email for advice. Be careful with this as it won't always work but, if a gatekeeper is willing to help you and has some sway with the decision-maker, it can be a good gamble.

Speaking to the decision-maker

Again, be polite and professional. You should also be conscious of the person's time, so don't spend valuable minutes waffling about yourself - remember, this is about the business. Mention your email then start to ask questions. It's very easy for a business owner to listen to you and then say they're not interested but, if you're asking well-informed questions, they have to interact.

Tailor your questions to the business and what you need to know but, if you're stuck, try some of these:

- » How did you get on at [EVENT] last weekend?
- » I saw you launched [PRODUCT], what's the response been like?
- » Have you ever thought about motorsport as a marketing tool?
- » Have you ever worked with influencers before?
- » I saw you worked with [INFLUENCER], how did that work out?
- » I love the new marketing campaign that's going out to [AUDIENCE], how did that come about?
- » I just wanted to give you a bit of an update on the email I sent, did you see it?

Don't spend a long time endlessly questioning the poor person, but one or two queries can open up those channels of communication to make the call more productive and less one-sided.

When to stop following-up

If you are consistently being ignored by a prospect, keep on at them. It might be that they're missing your emails, unable to reply or simply not interested but you'll never know which until you are able to speak to them.

I usually tell my clients to stop following up after they have a firm yes or no. Until then, don't give up.

32.

Tackling Price

Tackling price can be one of the trickiest parts of closing a sponsorship deal. I've heard from so many drivers who talk about positive email exchanges, only to have business baulk at the cost. There's a few reasons this is happening: the first could really be that they don't have the budget, but the more likely excuse is that they don't see value in what you're offering.

How your research can give you clues to budget

If you can go in understanding how much a sponsor is already spending on marketing, then you're well-placed to go in a with a price that seems reasonable. For example, if you've seen its ad in a magazine, you should use the skills you learnt in chapter 10 to find the rate card and see how much the business paid for that ad.

Bear in mind that businesses rarely pay full rate card prices for their ads as it's very easy to negotiate with a magazine advertising department, especially if you're able to take out a run of multiple ads.

It's also easy to find benchmark prices online for activity such as PR, video marketing, blog writing and events. The more you do this, the more you'll get a sense of what different activities cost.

You can also use websites such as Company Check to look for details of profit and loss, assets and debts. Getting an insight into the business's financials can help you to understand if it has money to spend, whether it's growing or whether to steer clear. Bear in mind that businesses often spend a lot of money before going through a growth period, and this might be reflected in their financials.

Qualifying phrases to use

Qualifying the buyer is so important, because it saves everyone some time and cuts straight to the chase. I can speak from experience as a business owner - if something is right for my business, I will find the money, but it's good to know if a decision-maker can do this before you spend your own money taking them to races or travelling to meetings.

A really straightforward qualifying question could be:

> "Based on what we've discussed, the costs for the package that will best suit your needs could be in the £5,000 to £10,000 range. How does that fit within your budget?"

Some prospects won't want to talk costs but, if you can get an idea of what kind of budget they have, you'll know whether or not you're wasting your time. At the very least, it's important to know if the business has some money to spend.

> "Is the revenue you'll get from the sales I could provide worth your time?"

For this to work, you already need an idea of how much a customer is worth to them. You need to be able to show that you can bring in real business benefit, because even brand awareness and PR will eventually lead to sales. Do your research - make sure you know how much a business is spending on advertising, the kind of events it attends and where its money is currently being spent. This will give you an idea of whether it's a £500 potential or a £5,000 potential.

"What's your timeline on this?"

The last thing you want is to find out the potential sponsor won't be able to make a decision for six months, part-way into your race season. This might be a prospect to nurture but not one to focus your efforts on now.

"Do you feel this adds value?"

When talking about your sponsorship packages, you want to know whether your prospect feels a partnership would be valuable. If the answer to this is positive, you're halfway there.

Why this is important for not wasting anyone's time

You could spend months grooming a lead without ever mentioning figures but, when it comes to signing on the dotted line, the business says it only has £1,000 to spend on the £50,000 package you've been pushing.

Qualify the buyer early on in the process, once they've shown some interest. This will save you time chasing leads that will ultimately go nowhere.

Tell them what you want in exchange for what you can offer

A lot of racing drivers make the mistake of asking the potential sponsor how much it would like to pay. This is without having any real understanding of how to show value to a sale prospect.

You wouldn't sell a product to a department store and ask it to tell you how much it's worth - you set the price.

Tell the sponsor how much the package is worth. If it really wants to work with you but can't afford the package cost, the negotiation process begins.

How to Negotiate

Business owners are savvy to sales tactics and many will want to negotiate; there's a few ways around this. Firstly, be very firm with your package costs and use definite language. Trust the value you can bring to a business and don't offer a discount unless it is struggling to make a decision.

So many racing drivers are quick to offer a discount before they've even worked out what the prospect is willing to pay. Only discount if you think it's the difference between a sale or no sale.

If you offer a package that you want £20,000 for but a business comes in offering £15,000, ask which parts of the package will be most valuable to it. Say you can do that price but you'll have to take out some of the less valuable stuff, such as standard race tickets for competitions.

If someone negotiates with you, give them one counter-offer. Obviously, how you counter depends on your relationship with the business and how much you need the money. Go with your gut but don't be greedy.

Do it face to face or on the phone

Face-to-face is the best way to negotiate, because you can pick up on a business owner's body language and tells. It's also much harder for them to say no to your proposal.

The next best solution would be to do it over the phone, as tone of voice says a lot about what's not being said.

Focus on the business' goals

Once again, when talking about price, focus on the business's goals and the value you can bring. If a business owner can see that this activity can bring them a return on investment, the money is almost a moot point.

Consistently focus on the value you can bring and the way that relates to a business's goals.

Wine and dine the owner

If you're looking to land a big sponsorship deal, it may take more than a few phone calls and meetings. You need to treat the potential sponsor like it's already on board and give it a taste of things to come. This can be a gamble because these things can still fall through.

> The best way to give a potential sponsor an insight into what you can offer would be to invite its team to a race or test day where they can rub shoulders with your existing sponsors.

Get used to talking about money and don't be afraid of it. Money is your friend, because it's going to make all your dreams come true.

33.

Closing the Sale

Closing the sale is the hardest part of any sales process. Everyone seems happy, they're excited about what you're doing and see real value in it - you just need them to say a definite yes to the package and the costs. That shouldn't be as difficult as it sounds, but it often is.

Get down to the real objection

"We don't have enough budget" usually means, "we're not sure this will add value". Ask questions to get down to the real reasons the prospect is unsure about buying.

Listen

Customers will often tell you when they're ready to buy - make sure you listen. Too many people miss these indicators because they're waffling away about themselves.

Sometimes it's obvious when a sponsor is ready. One of the sponsors for this book told me on our very first call: "This is exciting and we'd like to go ahead." That was very easy to close, because all I had to do was say "OK" and prepare a contract.

Other times, the business owner might be more subtle. Listen out for positive phrases such as:

- » "This will definitely help our business."
- » "I think we should give this a go."
- » "What are the next steps?"
- » "You're offering a lot of value."
- » "Would you handle the contract?"
- » "What's the next race we could attend?"
- » "Would your car be ready for an event next month?"

Ask for the sale

When you think a buyer is ready, ask for the sale. It really is often that simple. Try something like:

- » "It seems like these two packages are the best options based on your goals. Which one would you like to move forward with?"
- » "It sounds like this package could really help you meet [specific goal]. Would you like to get started on the contract now?"
- » "It seems like this package satisfies all of the criteria you're looking for. We can get started now, or we can schedule another meeting if you want more time to investigate other options."
- » "If we could find a way to deal with [objection], would you sign the contract on [set period in time]?"
- » "Would you like my help?"

If you don't make the sale, make another appointment

Sometimes people need time to make a decision or they'll have to bring other people in to discuss it with. If they need this time, that's fine, but make sure to get another appointment while you're there - otherwise you'll be chasing and chasing.

34.

Signing the Contract

A contract is an integral part of any sponsorship deal, especially if you're asking for money to be paid monthly or per race. Unfortunately, some businesses will try to get out of paying you. If you're working hard for company and it's getting results, you'll be fine, but it's best to have a contract in place to cover yourself and ensure you get paid for the work you're doing.

You can find simple sponsorship contract templates online which will give you a good starting point but, if you're working on a very large sponsorship deal - especially one with multiple payments - speak to a professional.

While my experience writing contracts within my marketing business and Racing Mentor has served me well, I am far from an expert. I felt you'd get more from this section if it were written by someone who knows the ins and outs of motorsport's legal system.

Genevieve Gordon-Thomson is a sports lawyer and CEO of Tactic Connect, a bespoke sports consultancy. She recently wrote the world's first Masters Programme, *Business of Motorsport,* which has been launched at De Montfort University. She also teaches International Sports Law and Global Sports Marketing at universities in the UK and USA. Because of this, she's well placed to lay out some starting points below.

Basic legalities of sponsorship

The basic principles of contract law cover the role of sponsorship in sports. You should be able to refer to your contract and understand your obligations with relevant ease.

There are many elements of a contract to consider when drafting them for clients and, below, you will be able to see the most common areas of a basic sponsorship contract that need consideration when developing sponsor relationships.

Who are the parties

Although this may sound obvious, it is important that parties to the contract are identified and named. You should know whether you are entering a contract with a company (incorporated or unincorporated) or an individual. It isn't always that obvious, so do take care to know who exactly you are contracting with. Note that companies can often trade as other names and they can also be subsidiaries of other companies. Who you think you are engaging with may turn out to be someone completely different - what is key is that the entity has a legal personality.

Written agreement

A contract can become very hard to enforce if you rely on performance or part-performance - therefore, agreements should be converted into a formal written (and signed) document. Forming a written document makes providing the existence of the terms much easier and should make it simpler to establish the required certainty in the terms of the contract.

Negotiation

Negotiation is a critical element of any sponsorship agreement, whether it revolves around motorsport, sport or another industry. Negotiating your own terms can be daunting and it is perfectly okay to ask someone to negotiate on your behalf. Quite often, it is a lot easier to nominate someone to act on your behalf.

Negotiation can take months, but it is important to hang on in there and secure a deal that you are comfortable with. In my experience, if you don't, you won't have a happy relationship with your sponsor.

My top tip would be to ask someone you can trust to negotiate on your behalf, and doesn't have a vested interest in you and your achievements. It is important that the person you ask to negotiate on your behalf knows and understands the market, understands your personal goals and overall aims so that they can negotiate effectively and in good time without having to revert to you at every point of discussion.

Define key words

Clearly define important, technical, abbreviated or oft-repeated terms. By doing this, you can all be sure of the meanings of each of the terms for the purposes of the contract at hand. Be precise and forward-thinking when defining words used to structure the terms of a contract.

Rights and obligations

Consider such matters as the rights and obligations of the parties, the length/time of the contract, options for renewal and payment terms. For example, imagine a typical sponsorship agreement in which you are obliged to wear a certain manufacturer's clothing when competing or training. Does the contract relate solely to a particular country or location? What does the word 'clothing' include? Maybe the sponsor envisages clothing in its entirety, whereas you don't.

Territory

What will be the territory to which the contract relates - i.e. the political and/or geographical area? The law usually uses national or worldwide based definitions of territory. Territorial definition may influence the workability of a contract if you are intending to travel within your sport.

Rights

Various different rights exist for the benefit of commercial exploitation. The division of rights and corresponding obligations is a highly important legal and economic area for the sports industry. Be very clear about your Image Rights and Intellectual Property - you may be agreeing to allow your IP to be used for the duration of the agreement. Be sure to clearly identify what can and can't be used and by whom. This is also an ideal opportunity to consider what happens to images of you once your agreement has been concluded.

Termination

Contracts can be for an indefinite period of time, but it is normal to specify a date and time when the contract will conclude. There may be a notice provision which is exercisable by either party to end the contract. The contract may also include terms that service termination, such as restrictive covenants; for example, you may not be able to work with a rival organisation for a period of time after the contract has ended. Restrictive covenants may or may not be enforceable, depending on the jurisdiction of the contract and the facts - however, it is important that you understand the implications of termination clauses.

Payment

Contracts vary enormously when types of payment are considered. Payments can be a combination of methods but will likely be determined by industry standards and customs of the sport. It's key to ensure tax payments are allocated to one party or other.

Variation and breach

Both parties to the contract should agree, in writing, to any variations and addendums to the contract, as one party cannot unilaterally vary a contract that has been negotiated. Breach of contract will happen when one party refuses to perform or vary the obligations agreed to. This type of behaviour will entitle the other party to damages and, in some cases, termination of contract.

Undue influence

Undue influence amounts to unequal pressure by one party to another, and is often presumed in contracts relating to minors and vulnerable adults. The terms of the contract should be 'reasonable'. The minor must have access to independent advice in respect to the terms agreed in the contract. If no independent advice has been received and the terms of the contract are unreasonable, the contract could be considered unfair and deemed unenforceable. It is important to note that adults can also be persuaded to agreeing terms they would not normally accept, and should be just as aware of the influencers surrounding their 'deals.'

Exclusivity

Be very aware of exclusivity within a contract. Are you wanting to contractually oblige yourself to one company only, or would you like to be able to have a number of sponsors that benefit from different elements of your personality and access to your sport?

Final thoughts

Contracting parties entering into agreements are capable of omitting or failing to add basic clauses into the contract - perhaps because they do not anticipate the potential changes in choice circumstances that may affect them. Disputes arise from ill-conceived or poorly-drafted contracts and do occur even if the parties have a history of goodwill and fair conduct between one another. Disputes also arise because of lack of commercial and legal awareness or insufficient preparation and attention to detail.

My own experience has shown preparing to succeed may take some time and a little outlay, but that is nothing compared to the misfortune you may find yourself in should you not invest your time and money wisely.

A final note is worthy here: contracts are often formed subject to sports governance rules and regulations and, therefore, it is highly advisable to consider and understand the relevant rules and regulations of any governing body when entering into sports contracts.

PART FIVE

WORKING WITH SPONSORS

Let's face it: landing the sponsorship deal is the hardest part of working with sponsors but, once you've got a brand on board, you want to work hard for them so they stick around for years to come.

This section can serve as your guidebook for working with an existing sponsor or inspiration for building a sponsorship package.

If the latter, remember to work out the benefits of all these activities based on the information in chapter 24.

35.

Your Responsibility Before the Race Weekend

Find out what sponsors need in terms of tickets, hospitality and photo/video content so you can be prepared - the last thing you want to do is go into a race weekend with sponsors making demands you hadn't planned for.

If this is a race where you need a big hospitality offering, then bear in mind that this will take some organising. If you don't have hospitality at every race weekend, you'll need to know well ahead of time specific numbers and dietary requirements.

Social updates

In order to create a buzz about your racing, you should be posting on all your social channels about the upcoming race weekend: where are you in the championship? What does this race mean to you? Are you looking forward to it? What sponsors will you have there?

Post pictures of car prep, packing, your race suit and anything else you can think of that will show off not only what you're doing, but also get your sponsors' logos in front of more people. Perhaps even record a short vlog about what you expect from the weekend, how you're trying a new nutrition plan or anything else relevant that you've been working on.

Where possible, your social updates can encourage people to go along to the races, visit your garage and say hello. All of this is great for your presence at a race track.

You should also tease any special events and competitions that are taking place during the weekend. Mention any relevant sponsors in these posts, too.

Posting regularly is a great way to increase your engagement and reach more people - good news for both you and your sponsors. Plus, if you've worked hard to build your audience, they'll want to know what you're up to.

Blog updates

It's good practice to write up a race preview, which can also serve as an update of any other activity. Updating your blog regularly is also great for your visibility in the search engines and will draw more readers your way.

Consider covering:

- » Any recent activity you've undertaken with your sponsors
- » A reminder of how your last race went
- » Any changes to the car or livery
- » Any new sponsor announcements (although, these should probably have a separate blog post too)
- » How you feel about the upcoming race weekend
- » What you think might be challenging
- » What you're looking forward to
- » How people can find you there
- » Any special events for your audience and how people can get involved

Communicate with sponsors

As well as the usual communication you'd have with your team, it's also important to communicate with sponsors. This is especially important if the sponsor is sending along any guests, running a competition or getting directly involved with your weekend in another way.

If you're unsure what you should be doing before a race weekend (save for visualising the track and prepping for the actual racing), look back through the package details you sent to your sponsor. If you're not doing much work for sponsors yet, consider what work you could do to continue building your profile and attracting businesses that might be interested in working with you.

36.

Your Responsibility on Race Day

A longside kicking butt on the race track, you need to think about looking after your sponsors and fulfilling your end of any agreement. This can make race day very busy so it's always good to have help on hand, be that promotional staff or family and friends.

Hospitality

When you have guests in hospitality, it's good form to stop by between races to say hello and shake a few hands. However, if you're having a crazy weekend, guests will understand that you can't be there all the time.

When you get a moment, pop in and make sure your guests are being looked after. Answer any questions about the racing and, if you can, offer VIP sponsors the chance to get up close with the car.

Q&As

A question and answer session is a great way to give guests and sponsors a real insight into the world of a racing driver and quickly familiarise them with the car and racing. If you can make this a rare, money-can't-buy experience, it's something really valuable to offer as a driver.

A good time to do your Q&A is during a lunch break or in the evening on a Saturday, once all the racing is over. You could also take your guests on a track walk, if time and circuit rules allow.

Networking

If your sponsors are bringing important guests to a race, there's a chance that these guests could be potential sponsors or introduce you to some. It's important to look after your sponsor's interests first but, also, take your time to network.

Making guests feel special

A bit of personal attention from an important racing driver can go a long way to making guests feel special. If you're interacting directly with your sponsors, it's a good chance to build that relationship. If your sponsor has sent guests along (customers, prospects, competition winners, suppliers or employees), you should treat them as you would your sponsor.

If you look after these people, it'll get back to your sponsor, further strengthening the relationship.

Social updates

If you can find the time, post a few updates to social media. Being visible to your audience is really important and they'll want an insight into your racing. You could always enlist the help of a team member or friend to help you with your social posts. Here are some ideas for engaging content:

- » Live Facebook video at the end of each day, updating your audience
- » Video content introducing one of your sponsors - either an interview with a key employee or a product review

- » Photographs of your race car and you looking race-ready
- » Photographs of weather conditions, the track, your hospitality area, etc.
- » Live race updates
- » Information on how you're working with sponsors during the race weekend
- » Behind-the-scenes posts, video and images showing how the team works together

Photography

It's really important that you have someone taking professional photos during each race weekend. Luckily, there are always photographers around and, usually, all you have to do is spend a little money on a disc of images at the end of the weekend.

Depending on what kind of agreement you have with your sponsor, you may need slightly more specialist photos. It's all well and good getting some on-track photos, but it's also important to get some candid shots of you with your team, interacting with guests and getting ready to race.

After all, people want to see you just as much as they want to see your race car.

A roaming photographer might not have the time to spend all day in your garage, so consider hiring a photographer or paying a little more money to have someone follow you around for a few hours.

Video

Video content is also important during a race weekend, especially if you have a YouTube channel that draws a large audience. Again, enlist the help of a friend or family member, or consider hiring a professional to handle the camera for you.

While in-car footage is a great way to show people how your race weekend went, think about doing something a little different. Again, it's important to stand out from the crowd, so experiment with different kinds of videos from vlogs, to skits, to real insights into the life of a racing driver.

Here are some ideas, but take time to brainstorm some of your own if video is important to you:

- » Choosing tyres during a wet race
- » How to get in the zone before a race
- » Introducing a new sponsor with an interview
- » Being interviewed by a fellow racer
- » What a racing driver eats before a race
- » How a racing driver warms up before a race
- » How you use a sponsor's product during a race weekend

Speaking to the press

If you win a race you will be expected to, at the very least, speak to a commentator or pitlane reporter. You may even end up on TV if your series has coverage. If you're racing in the big leagues you'll be used to speaking to the press, but it always helps to enhance your skills.

I worked with a very polite, well-spoken young racing driver who was more than happy to talk in front of the camera but he babbled, tried too hard to answer the question and lacked energy because he was focussing was too much.

Ask him the same questions in any other situation and he was full of energy; he just needed to relax. The same thing goes for most racing drivers who don't come across well on camera - if you can relax, you'll instantly seem more natural.

Here's the process I take my drivers through when they struggle in front of the camera:

» **Think of a time when you did well** - Remember the adrenaline, the excitement. Smile. Really feel it, then hang onto that feeling so it's easy to conjure up later

» **Relax** - Take a few deep breaths

» **Identify any anxieties** - Notice them then just brush them to one side

» **Stay on topic** - Answer the question with as much detail as you want but, once it's answered, don't keep talking. The journalist will then ask their next question

» **Relax** - This goes for your mind and body. You don't want to be stiff but you don't want to be fidgeting either

» **Show emotion** - Your facial expressions can say a lot. Smile when you're happy, make eye contact, laugh

» **Relax** - You've got this

Tom Chilton is a face I enjoy seeing on television because he's always positive and relaxed. I spoke to him about how racing drivers could maximise their presence in front of the press; he said: "Media training is key for all drivers. How to present yourself and get the key messages out is what it's all about. You need to keep the sponsors happy - after all, you're the face of it to them."

As well as television and circuit press, you should seek out other journalists covering the race weekend; the easiest way is to do this on social media. Look for press who are talking about the event and send them messages to see if they'd like to interview you. Again, like any PR activity, you need a hook: why should they write about you over any of the other drivers there?

If you've been getting regular press coverage, you'll already have good contacts with journalists at races. Make sure to meet with these people in person when you can and invite them along to your garage. Maybe even offer them lunch in your hospitality.

Getting a sponsor's name out there

There are a number of ways you can get your sponsor's name out there at a race weekend. Make sure you're photographed in your race suit and captured on TV in a branded cap. Thank your sponsors when giving interviews, or mention you're hosting guests from the business in your hospitality.

Also include your sponsors in social updates, mention them by name in video content and make sure their logo is visible in any pictures you post.

37.

Following the Race Weekend

Once the race weekend is over, you need to take some time to relax and recover - but there's also work to be done.

Write a Race Report

If you've agreed with sponsors that you'll be sending a report after every race, you need to do this in a timely manner - usually on the Monday or Tuesday following the race. If you're not used to writing this kind of content it might take you some time, but persevere - you'll soon get used to it.

A race report should have the same kind of format as a press release. Hook the reader with main points in the first line and then go into more detail as you move through the report. Make sure to write it all in third person, and include a quote from yourself that could be easily lifted for an article on a sponsor's website or in a magazine.

Make sure to also thank your sponsors towards the end of the piece.

This report will serve as an article that can be posted by sponsors as well as a press release that will go out to your PR contacts.

Sending media

Again, if you've agreed with sponsors to send pictures within a certain time frame, you need to make sure you fulfil this promise. Sometimes you might have to wait for photographers to get the pictures to you, but make sure to communicate this to your sponsor if that's the case.

The easiest way to send photos and videos from your weekend is with Dropbox, as they'll automatically get uploaded to a folder that you and all your sponsors have access to.

Following up with guests

If you've spoke to sponsors and their guests at a race weekend, make sure to follow up to make sure they had fun. This is a really important part of relationship-building, as it'll make the sponsor feel valued.

Other deliverables

Your agreement with your sponsor might include other deliverables, such as specific social media posts, exclusive quotes about the weekend or video blogs aimed at its audience.

Make sure you know exactly what you should be delivering to your sponsors before, during and after the race event. This keeps them on your side and happy, which is important when it comes to renewing the deal at the end of the year.

38.

Between Races

The work doesn't stop between events, especially if you're a brand ambassador. Of course, you need to focus on your fitness and race craft, but there's plenty you need to do for sponsors, too.

Working with sponsors at events

It's likely that, as part of a large sponsorship agreement, you'll be required to attend sponsor events. This might be as simple as showing your face at a business breakfast, or it could be something a little larger that takes more planning, such as a trade show or conference where you're required to do a talk.

Whatever the event, remember that you are there representing your sponsor. Some events are likely to be more interesting than others but it's this work that keeps you racing. Smile, enjoy talking to people, sell your sponsor, talk about the exciting life of a racing driver and have fun.

Getting your car to events

A race car at an event is a big draw for the crowds. It can act as a talking point and will be photographed thoroughly, no matter what the event is. This is fantastic social media coverage for any brand.

In your contract with a sponsor, you should specify how the costs of car transport will work. As part of the sponsorship deal, are you just making your car available and happy to transport it, but the sponsor has to pay extra for fuel, trailer hire and whatever else you need?

Or are you absorbing the costs from a large sponsorship sum to cover a certain amount of events per year? Make sure you understand how this will work with your sponsor so you're not left out of pocket (and make sure it's part of a contract so both parties know what to expect).

Social media

Just because you're not racing doesn't mean you don't have anything to post about. Keep your audience up-to-date with events you're attending, any test days you're taking part in and anything else you think might interest them. Remember, you don't have to be business all day every day - let some personality shine through. Post about your dog walk on the beach, or take a photo of some amazing street art you saw on your run.

Don't forget that people are buying into *you*.

Images and videos do particularly well on social media, so make sure to keep up with your posting schedule to please sponsors and keep your audience engaged.

If you need to take a break during the week, spend some time scheduling posts to go out automatically. You might need to check in on your social channels to reply to comments and messages, but it'll save you a lot of time thinking up things to post on the fly.

For the Racing Mentor social accounts, I schedule posts, videos and images one-to-two weeks ahead of time but, if I've got something happening in the moment, I make sure to also post that.

Scheduled posts are great for sponsor plugs, images from your racing or announcements of events, but don't be afraid to let the world know what you're doing as it happens. What you post completely depends on your brand and the niche you've created for yourself.

For scheduling I use Buffer, which covers Twitter, Facebook, LinkedIn and Instagram. It's free with paid plans.

Press coverage

Press coverage is your secret weapon in building your profile and attracting sponsors but, just because you've landed a sponsor, you shouldn't rest on your laurels.

Getting press coverage is important for you and your sponsors. If you've created your race report following the race and sent it out to your press contacts, you need to follow up. Ask your contacts if they need images or further information.

You should also keep an eye out for other press opportunities. Look for stories you could comment on either as a racing driver or as a brand ambassador.

The information at Racingmentor.com/PR will give you some ideas.

39.

How to Get Help with All of This

This is obviously a lot of work for one driver to do alone, but there are people and services out there that can help you. Obviously, as a person who provides these kinds of services to racing drivers, I'm biased.

If you are looking for someone to take the reins, I have this advice.

- » Find a good communicator who you can trust
- » Meet the person face-to-face or at least on a video call
- » Where possible, make sure you sign a contract, even if you have to provide it
- » Get your agreement over email so everyone knows what to deliver
- » Avoid people willing to work for free as there's a chance it could result in you letting down sponsors
- » Make sure the person you employ has to right contacts and skills
- » Ask for testimonials and references
- » Bear in mind that an agency will often charge more than a freelancer

» Ask fellow racers for recommendations

If you're interested in what Racing Mentor offers in this arena, take a look at Racingmentor.com/bookoffers for some special deals.

Your time is precious and I'm guessing you're in this industry to have fun and race some cars. It's very easy to get so bogged down with sponsorship activities that you don't get the chance to enjoy your racing: don't let this happen. Don't lose the love. Ask for help when you need it and farm out some of the more time-consuming tasks to a friend, family member or freelancer.

That's enough of a sales pitch from me. Onto the next chapter!

40.

Acting as a Brand Ambassador

A brand ambassador is paid to promote a company's products and services to their audience. Doing this as a racing driver is an important part of any sponsorship deal. If these companies are willing to pay bloggers, celebrities, reality TV stars and sports people to promote their products, why not a racing driver, too?

Your role as a brand ambassador will vary depending on what you've agreed with a sponsor, but there's usually two sides to it: making your sponsor look good by talking about its business in the press, and directly promoting its products to your audience.

Giving comment to the press

It's dull to always have your CEO give comment to the press, so why not have an exciting brand ambassador do it? Whatever you're commenting on - a new product, legislation in the industry, an event or other relevant news - it makes the sponsor look good to have someone well-known and influential do it.

If a CEO is talking about how great their product is, everyone will take that with a pinch of salt but, if people see a racing driver promoting something, they're likely to take it a bit more seriously.

The press are also very interested in celebrity, so your presence within a release could be the hook they need to run a story.

Being a Spokesperson

Being a spokesperson for a business or charity means that the press will often come to you for quotes. You'll need to work closely with your sponsor on this to make sure you're on-message. In many cases, you'll be acting as the voice and face of the brand (this is a big deal, so the amount of sponsorship you receive in return should reflect this).

Promoting the sponsor at sponsor events

When you go to a sponsor's event you can't just talk about yourself, nor can you stand in a corner and only eat the free food - it's your job at these events to talk to people, make yourself known and speak positively of the brand you're working with.

You need to know the brand and its products or services inside-out, as well as understanding the kind of people you'll be meeting. If you're unsure of what you're supposed to be doing, speak to your contact at the business as they'll no doubt be very happy to give you some product training if it helps you make them more sales.

Promoting the sponsor outside of your racing life

One of the biggest benefits of teaming up with a business that's relevant to your non-racing life (if you have such a thing) is that you can promote it away from the race track.

This might mean getting a watch sponsor to complement your day job in the fashion industry, or it could mean working with a food delivery service as part of your work as a food blogger.

Even if you just have the sway within your day job to get your sponsor's product in front of the right people at your company, this can be an important benefit to a business.

One racing driver I used to work with employed a lot of people in his day job so, when he started working with a recruitment company sponsor, those employees got direct real-world benefit from his non-racing work.

Social media

A good way to act as a brand ambassador on social media is to show how you've used a sponsor's products.

- » Use photo or video to show you installing a sponsor's air filter
- » Talk about how you feel so much more awake in the mornings thanks to a sponsor's energy drink
- » Ask questions about what people wear during their evening yoga class, then mention that you wear leggings from your sponsor's new fitness range
- » Maybe even mention how a sponsor's oil has made your race car run so much smoother

Don't force this content. If you're working with the right company, this should come quite naturally.

Being natural

The general public has become blind to advertising, which is why so many brands rely on influencers to promote their products.

But there's only so much we can take from all the Instagrammers out there (I decided not to call them 'Instagram stars' because I think that's stretching celebrity a little far) promoting coffee scrubs, tanning products, fitness retreats, health foods, planners, books, noisy exhaust systems, marketing platforms, hiking boots and whatever else is the product du jour.

If you love and trust an influencer, you're probably going to buy whatever they're helping to sell but, because there are so many people doing this - especially on Instagram - we wonder who we can trust.

For you to be successful in your role as an influencer and brand ambassador, you need to truly love a product to promote it naturally.

You also need to build trust within your audience before you start blindly selling to them. If you can understand what they want to buy, you're more likely to make sales for the sponsors that fund your racing career.

41.

Continuing to Grow Your Audience

Just because you've landed a few good sponsors, it doesn't mean you shouldn't continue to grow your audience. It's likely that all your activity landing and working with sponsors will generate enough content and coverage to keep your audience growing naturally, but don't neglect your duties to the people who follow you.

Working with your sponsor to grow both your audiences

While you'll talk about how your audience can benefit a business, don't forget that there's huge benefit to you in working with a high-profile sponsor. It'll give you more reach and influence, so consider this when pitching to different companies.

Again, the joint activity you do with your sponsor will naturally help you reach a wider audience, but consider these activities for boosting your reach alongside the work you're doing to give your sponsor access to your audience:

> » Regular blog posts on the sponsor's website - It gets content while you reach its audience

» Speaking gigs - You can mention your sponsor but you're also telling the audience about yourself

» Social media takeovers - Your followers may follow the sponsor to take part, but some of the sponsor's audience may follow you too

» Asking the sponsor to post and retweet - Not only is it good for its brand image, but you can tap into its audience, too

Building more value for the future

Ensuring you continue to build your audience is so important because, in the coming years, you're probably going to need more sponsorship to get where you want to be. As your audience becomes more valuable, the amount of sponsorship you can ask for will go up.

This is something to mention to sponsors early on in your career. You can talk about how you're growing your audiences (mention numbers here, i.e. 100% follower growth on Twitter in the last month) and how it's good for a sponsor to come on board at this time. It will get first access to this audience without paying premium prices.

This is a good way to get a tentative sponsor on board, but make sure not to over-promise and under-deliver, even if the business is only paying a few hundred pounds.

PART SIX

REVIEWING, REPORTING AND RENEWING

Throughout any business relationship, it's important to continually check-in to ensure your client is happy - the same is true in the racing driver-sponsor relationship. If you can check in to make sure your sponsors are happy, you're more likely to get them to renew for another year.

It also gives you a sense of what you're doing right - and, sometimes, what you're doing wrong. This means you have a good basis to improve for both existing and future sponsors.

Reporting also has huge benefit to you as well as to your sponsor. A report, even a simple one, shows a sponsor how hard you're working for it, but the stats you get are fantastic for convincing potential sponsors what you're worth.

42.

The Importance of Reviewing Regularly

In order to keep a sponsor happy, you need to review regularly. This is the best way to monitor everyone's activity, input and performance. It can be difficult to hear that a sponsor isn't happy but, if you can fix whatever is going on, you're more likely to be able to get that sponsor to renew in the future.

Asking if your sponsors are happy

The easiest way to do this is to ask if your sponsor is happy - if the business is enjoying the attention, seeing the benefits and getting good reports from customers and employees, then that's fantastic.

However, just because a sponsor is happy doesn't mean there isn't something you could be doing better. Regardless of its answer, you still need to ask this next question.

Asking what you can do better

This is so important for a good ongoing relationship. Firstly, it shows the business that you actually care how your work impacts it, but it can also help you to make more of an impact.

Some sponsors might be a bit irrational and complain about

how they're not making 5,000% more sales after only giving you £500, so watch out for anyone who is asking too much. More rational sponsors might mention how well a certain type of tweet worked for them and ask if you can do more. Some might say they were disappointed you didn't get to greet their guests at the last race; some might say they're happy and ask if they can do anything more to assist you.

Don't let people take advantage of you, but do take these concerns seriously. You could always incorporate the more difficult or time-consuming ideas into a larger sponsorship package for the following year.

Asking for an update on sales/impact of your work

Evidence of how sponsorship is benefiting a business is a vital tool in future sponsorship pitches; ask a sponsor to provide some kind of indication as to how the sponsorship activity is affecting its goals and bottom line.

Some might not want to or might not be able to give specific numbers, but can still give you a yes or no. Others might be able to give you a percentage increase of sales that's been helped by your activity. Any stats relating to sales are hugely valuable when you pitch to new sponsors in the future, as well as when you come to renew your existing sponsorship deals.

You might also get stats on social followers, engagement, customer happiness, press coverage and more. A stat I like to promote to potential sponsors is the value of press coverage, which we've already touched on earlier in this book.

If you can show any potential sponsor that you brought £30,000 of press coverage to a single partner during the previous race season, it seems like a no-brainer.

Even better, show an existing sponsor that you brought it £30,000 worth of press coverage and it would be silly not to renew. More often than not, sponsors will count pieces of coverage but they won't look at equivalent advertising value. Your coverage count might sound impressive, but the monetary value sounds even better.

43.

Regular Reports

Sending regular reports to your sponsors also gives them a insight into your activity. Let's assume that, in the first few months of your partnership, your activity hasn't yet made a difference to a sponsor's sales - that's normal; these things take time.

If you're not updating your sponsor with what you've been working on, it could safely assume you're not doing anything and are failing to fulfil your part of the agreement.

But, if you're sending reports or at least updating with a short email, the sponsor is going to see how hard you're working.

How often?

This depends on how much work you're doing for your sponsor. I'd say that monthly is fine, but don't be afraid to send emails or messages whenever you land a piece of coverage or have a lead to send its way.

What to Include

Again, this depends on what you're doing but, I'd include a combination of the following:

- » What you've done for your sponsor
- » Events attended
- » PR coverage achieved
- » Most popular social posts
- » Social reach on posts promoting your sponsor
- » Videos filmed/in progress
- » Other ideas
- » Goals for next month
- » Preview of next month's activity
- » Key dates (races, events, test days, etc.)
- » Race results

Stats

Statistics are important - these are proof that your activity is working. The easiest stats to get hold of are the social and PR ones that we covered in Part I of this book.

If you've hosted an event or have been speaking with sales managers, you may also have stats on sales. Feel free to include these, too, as they're often a good indicator of your direct impact.

Testimonials

If you report to the marketing manager but also work closely with sales staff, get testimonials from them on your work. For example, if you're working the floor at a trade show and a manager is impressed with how you drew people to the stand, get a testimonial about this work, otherwise the marketing manager or CEO (i.e. the person with the power to renew at the end of the year) may never know.

The same goes for guests at any events you host. Speak to your sponsor's guests and, if you really create a rapport with someone, ask for a two-line testimonial about their hospitality experience.

This is all powerful information when renewal time comes around and you need to tell a sponsor why it should continue to work with you.

44.

Renewing Sponsorship

A lot of racing drivers seem to struggle to renew a sponsor after a year, and this is usually because they're not bringing enough value to that business. If you've followed all the advice in this book, you probably won't struggle to keep a sponsor on board for another year, but this chapter covers how to give yourself the best chance possible

For those of you who have just picked up this book but are eager to get an existing sponsor to renew, read this chapter carefully to give yourself the best chance of landing support for another year.

Why should a sponsor renew?

When you go into your renewal pitch, you need to give the sponsor clear reasons why you should continue to work together. By this point, you should have plenty of information on what's working and how your audience is reacting.

Some ideas:

- » Capitalise on the brand awareness built in the first year of partnership
- » Continue to reach a varied audience of potential customers

- » Reach a new audience with a move into [higher race series]
- » Increased press coverage thanks to a partnership with [magazine partner]

Why should the business continue working with you? You need to answer this question convincingly, but the fact that the partnership has already been working for the business and its bottom line is a valid enough reason.

Give relevant stats and activity

You need to give statistics and numbers, much in the same way you did when you first pitched. Talk about your follower numbers and reach, as these will have grown, and recalculate the value of your press coverage.

You can also talk about relevant stats from your work with the sponsor - for example, how many people have been reached during the partnership (looking at reach from all the social posts where you've mentioned the business).

If possible, you should also gather stats and testimonials from people within the business. This might be number of leads picked up from an event, direct sales figures or simply some kind words about your work.

All this is proof that your sponsorship efforts have had a real benefit to the business.

Do everything face-to-face

It's much harder for someone to say no to you in person. It's also much easier for you to sell when you can read someone's body language and facial expressions for clues.

Make sure you're looking at renewals before the final race of the season to give your sponsors time to make their decision.

Pin them down for a meeting where you can go through your updated figures, their sales stats and plans for next year's activity.

Don't put all your eggs in one basket

While it's important to look after existing partners, don't just assume they'll continue to fund your racing career. Even if you've worked wonders for them and have a good relationship, that's no guarantee that they'll continue the partnership.

Businesses are weird, organic things that don't always make sense - kind of like humans, I guess. It's important to hedge your bets and start looking elsewhere, just in case something happens that means you won't get that sponsorship money next year.

Start looking for new or additional sponsorship when you've still got a couple of races to go. The benefit of this is that you'll be able to invite potential new sponsors along to a race to get a feel of what it's all about.

If you're feeling stuck when it comes to giving a convincing renewal pitch, go back to the pitching section of this book. If all the stats and numbers are giving you a headache, return to basics and let the business buy into you and your personality once again.

"To finish first,
first you must finish."
- Rick Mears

The following pages include resources, further reading and a glossary for those of you who want to a dive a bit deeper into sponsorship, discover tools to make your life easier and explore more of what Racing Mentor has to offer.

Don't see this as the end, though. This is your motorsport sponsorship guide and the kind of book that can be referred back to time and time again.

I want to hear how you're getting on, so feel free to share your sponsorship wins with me at jess@racingmentor.com.

Now go out and land the biggest sponsorship deal of your life.

Resources

For a regularly-updated list of resources that will help you in your sponsorship search, visit Racingmentor.com/resources. There you'll find links to all the courses, books and other resources listed below.

Downloadables

Email checklist

A free Racing Mentor download that gives you a simple checklist of things you need to do before sending a pitch email.

Sponsorship email templates

A set of Racing Mentor pitch templates for hot, warm and cold leads as well as follow ups and phone scripts.

Guide to local PR

A free Racing Mentor guide to picking up press coverage in local newspapers and magazines.

Racing Mentor courses

The Sponsorship Bootcamp

This is a basic course on sponsorship. It's very similar to this book, but takes you step-by-step through crafting your first pitch.

The Ultimate Guide to PR

This is an in-depth course that will teach you how to find high-value press coverage to help you land a sponsorship deal.

Helpful Racing Mentor pages

Racingmentor.com/socialreach

More details on how to work out your social reach

Racingmentor.com/PR

A closer look at PR and how you can use it as a racing driver

Racingmentor.com/SEO

A deeper dive into search engine optimisation.

Racingmentor.com/research

Find research tips and templates here.

Racingmentor.com/adresearch

A video showing how you can find sponsors from magazine adverts.

Racingmentor.com/bookoffers

Offers from Racing Mentor and our partners.

Other helpful books

Four-Hour Work Week - Tim Ferriss

This book changed my whole outlook on business. For racers, it's valuable because it teaches you to become more productive. It may also inspire you to set up a side hustle to pay for your racing.

Sales Bible - Jeffrey Gitomer

I pick up this book whenever I need a reminder of how to qualify a buyer or deal with an objection. It's a fantastic book for beginners and experienced sales people alike.

Exit Strategy - Ellory Wells

For those of you looking to quit the daily grind and set up something that complements your racing career, this book will help you plan a realistic exit strategy.

You're a Badass at Making Money - Jen Sincero

This is a book about changing your mindset to money and allowing it to flow to you. It might sound a bit daft, but it's fantastic at helping you get over any mental blocks that might be stopping you reaching your potential.

Apps and tools

SupaPass

This is a company that can help you to launch your own subscription app. If you already have a large audience and want a way to monetise it, this is a good place to start.

Buffer

This is my social scheduling tool of choice.

Sprout Social

This is a powerful social media tool that allows you to manage all accounts from one place. It includes powerful analytics tools, but the best thing is the information it gives you on the people who follow you. Great for understanding your audience or researching sponsors.

Hubspot

This is a customer relationship management and sales tool. There's a free version that's great for keeping all of your pitches and sales processes in one place.

Boomerang

This is a Gmail add-on that allows you to schedule an email for sending later on; it's handy if you write an awesome pitch at 10pm but need to send it at 8am when it's more likely to get seen. It can also remind you to follow up on emails that haven't been replied to.

Hashme

This is a phone app that suggests relevant hashtags based on a topic. This is particularly helpful for Instagram.

Skype

An important tool for video calls.

Dropbox

A cloud storage tool that makes it easy for you to share images with sponsors or link to a pitch document, without clogging up a busy business owner's email inbox.

Xero

An easy way to create invoices for sponsors. It also makes things easier when it comes to working out your tax at the end of the year.

Clockify

A time tracking app that's useful if you've agreed on doing set hours of work per month for a sponsor.

Canva

A powerful tool that allows you to create your own graphics. Available both online and as an app.

Snapseed

A photo editing app that allows you to turn your phone photos into works of art. Great for tweaking an image before posting to social media.

Again, you can find links to all these resources at Racingmentor.com/resources

---

Glossary

A list of terms used throughout this book.

Audience

The group of people who follow what you do as a racing driver. The target audience of a sponsor is the people it wants to buy its products.

Brand ambassador

Someone who is paid to endorse a brand and promote its products or services.

Branding

The brand logos and messages that appear on your race car, suit, helmet, teamwear and digital presence.

Budget

The estimate of expenditure on specific activities. Sponsorship usually falls within a business's advertising or marketing budget.

Call-to-action

A piece of content designed to make the reader (or viewer, in the case of video) take a specific action. In this book, this usually means a line or two encouraging a potential sponsor to meet or hop on a call with you.

Customer engagement

The means by which a business creates a relationship with its customer base to foster brand loyalty and awareness.

Demographic

A group of people categorised by different factors such as age, income and/or location.

Domain Authority

This is a search engine ranking score that predicts how well a website will rank on search engine results pages.

Employee engagement

The means by which a business creates a relationship with its employees in order to retain talented staff.

Engagement

Businesses define this in a number of different ways. Ultimately it's the number of people interacting with your content.

Hashtag

A word or phrase preceded by a hash sign (#). Used on social media to identify messages on a specific topic.

Hook

The hook is something that draws a person in and makes them want to find out more.

Influencer

An influencer is someone whose authority is trusted by a specific audience.

Key performance indicator (KPI)

A measure used to evaluate the success of a project. Usually, an objective that needs hitting such as a certain number of sales.

Lead

This refers to contact with a potential customer. These can be broken down into hot leads, which are customers who've had a lot of contact with a business and are probably ready to buy; warm leads, those who know about the business but may need a bit more nurturing before they buy; and cold leads, those that seem to be good prospects but have yet to interact with the business.

Lead capture

The process of taking down a potential customer's details in order to sell to them in the future. This could be online or in person.

Lead magnet

A piece of content that acts as motivation for potential customers to hand over their email address or other contact information. These can be in the form of ebooks, checklists, reports, video courses or other incentives.

Niche

A position or activity that relates to a person's passions or talents.

Objections

The reason why a person might not buy.

Offering

The various things you, as a racing driver, can offer to potential sponsors. You use elements of your offering to build a sponsorship package.

Personal brand

The image you present to others about yourself and what you can offer to a company, its clients and your audience.

Pitch

A presentation of your idea to a potential sponsor. This can be done via email, on the phone, or in person.

Potential

This refers to a potential sponsor or potential customer. This is someone you think will benefit from your services.

Press outlet

Often referred to just as 'outlet' in this book. This is a magazine, newspaper, website, television channel, radio station, podcast or any other place you could get coverage.

Prospect

Another word for a potential customer or sponsor.

Qualifying questions

Questions that work out if the potential sponsor is ready to sign the contract. You may need a few of these as you go through the pitch process.

Rapport

The harmonious relationship you build with potential sponsors that helps you to understand one another and communicate effectively.

Reach

A social media stat that refers to the number of people who have come across a particular account or piece of content.

Return on investment (ROI)

A measure used to evaluate the efficiency of an investment.

Revenue

Another word for income.

Search engine optimisation (SEO)

The process of maximising the number of visitors to a website by ensuring it appears high in the list of results returned by a search engine.

Spokesperson

A person who makes statements (usually to the press) on behalf of a business.

Sponsorship proposal

Similar to a pitch, although this often refers to a designed document or slideshow that can be presented to potential sponsors.

Vlog

A shortened name for a video blog.

Acknowledgements

Firstly, this book wouldn't have happened without ambitious racing drivers like you. Keep up the good work.

Thank you to Ben Hastings for being endlessly patient with me during the writing phase of this book, and for bringing me food when I was on deadline. Thank you to Nell Walker for fulfilling BFF duties at all times, and also for proofreading my work and calling it 'wisdom'. And, while they may not have been actively involved in book production, thank you to Adam Johnson and Rose Reid for always having my back.

Thanks also need to go to my business coach, Ellory Wells, and the others in my mastermind group, Dane Gilson and Kris Cone. Thank you for your help, advice and support. I wouldn't be at this stage in my business if it wasn't for you.

Big car-filled thanks go to my motorsport crew, especially those who have given feedback in the Sponsorship Community on Facebook throughout the Racing Mentor journey. In particular I want to thank Rebecca Jackson for looking after me on a zipline in Wales and inspiring me to try new things.

Finally, I want to thank the sponsors and supporters of this book. Your support has been invaluable and I appreciate the belief you have in Racing Mentor and my vision.

About the Author

Jess Shanahan is a motorsport consultant and journalist. She set up Racing Mentor in 2016 to help racing drivers find sponsorship, and has since added consultancy services for motorsport businesses to her offering. The Racing Mentor project naturally came together due to her background in motorsport, most notably as a race team boss for Porsche outfit Turn Eight Racing, combined with more than 15 years' worth of marketing and PR experience.

Having grown up on the north Norfolk coast - and subsequently moving as far as Norwich - East Anglia is undoubtedly Jess's spiritual home, but she considers herself a digital nomad; she can be found working anywhere from the Austrian Alps, to a smart café in London or beside a race track. She is continually adding to her motoring knowledge with road tests and trips, contributions to racing discussions on radio and reviews of cars both on YouTube and on television.

When she's not behind the wheel – or helping out those that are – Jess plays board games, enjoys hiking and is learning German.

You can find Jess on Twitter and Instagram as both @jetlbomb and @RacingMentor. You can also follow the Racing Mentor Facebook page at Facebook.com/racingmentor.
